HEALTHY EATING FOR THE NEW AGE

The recipes in this book contain:

No animal flesh

No animal fats

No animal by-products

HEALTHY EATING FOR THE NEW AGE

A Vegan Cookbook

JOYCE D'SILVA

WILDWOOD HOUSE

For RONNIE LEE — *hopefully in liberation*

First published in Great Britain 1980
Reprinted 1981, 1984, 1986

Wildwood House Limited
Gower House
Croft Road
Aldershot
Hampshire GU11 3HR

ISBN 0 7045 0397 2

Typeset by Inforum Ltd, Portsmouth
Printed and bound in Great Britain by
The Camelot Press Ltd, Southampton

Contents

Foreword

As civilized human beings most of us have developed a rationale of mankind's acceptable behaviour towards the animal species, but our intellectual processes, and even our heart or spirit, might well have forced us into an ethical standpoint considerably beyond that by which we are prepared to live! Put in this position our defensive mechanism rationalizes and clouds the issue, but what really matters is where we each, as individuals, draw our frontier of actual practice, between the dictates of our conscience and the indulgence of our appetites.

The first step one might take along the road of conscientious limitation would be by adhering to 'wholefood' principles, and only eating meat from an animal which has lived a normal healthy open air life, ranging free in the fields. The two factors which are likely to have led up to this are considerations of nutritional value and flavour, and abhorrence of the 'factory farming' method where the animals are 'intensively' reared in conditions which could not possibly be condoned by any right thinking person who did in fact stop to look or think about it.

The next step is obviously 'lacto-vegetarianism', when meat is excluded from one's diet on humanitarian grounds, probably supported by the claim that many of the world's food shortages could be cured through the economy of land and energy resources that would result if meat production was phased out.

One might think that if the indulgent side of our nature has given ground as far as allowing us to eat vegetarian, then it is only a small step to eating according to 'vegan' principles! Vegan food is not only vegetarian, but also rules out the use of all dairy products on the perfectly logical premise that it is not enough to refuse to eat dead animals but that we should also refuse to exploit them when alive in the way that is necessary for the production of milk for human consumption. And let's face it, it does seem crazy and unnatural to base a large part of our food production on the milk a mother cow produces specially for her babies!

In fact even those who live entirely, or mainly, on vegetarian foods find the step to vegan foods a very difficult one, though they might well be persuaded as to the logic. Dairy produce has traditionally been the mainstay of a vegetarian diet, providing alternative protein and many of the vitamins and minerals needed for health. So that is why this recipe book of Joyce D'Silva can do such a valuable job in answering the oft repeated question 'Well it's difficult enough for a person living on vegetarian food, but for God's sake what's left for them to eat if they cut out milk, cheese and eggs?'!

I was asked, on behalf of Cranks, to write this Foreword because I think it was felt that we, as a vegetarian rather than a vegan organization could give a recommendation that was unbiased and would therefore carry more weight. I think and hope that this is true because I believe that the excellent and varied recipes which stick to health food as well as vegan principles will bring enjoyment to many, whether they be carnivore, vegetarian or vegan. At Cranks we already provide certain vegan foods and we are now delighted at the prospect of introducing some of Joyce D'Silva's exciting recipes into our repertoire.

David Canter
Cranks Health Foods

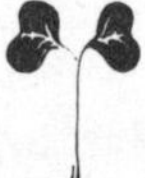

Acknowledgements

My thanks to my friends and to my mother, who allowed me to use their favourite vegan recipes. Special thanks to Deborah Singmaster and Jane Middleton for all their help and advice, and to Philip Williams for getting my manuscript copied. Thanks also to Christine Minton, Cathy Causton, Christine Seville and Philip Shore for their help and encouragement.

I am indebted to the Vegan Society for continuous inspiration and encouragement.

Most thanks of all to Amancio, who provided both help and some of the Indian recipes, and also cheerfully endured the endless tapping of my typewriter, and to our children Maria, Stephano and Francesca who have always been the best critics of my cooking! Not forgetting our feline friend Tiger, who tasted the left-overs and set her seal of approval on many of them.

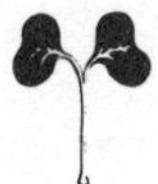

Introduction

As I sat down to work on this book, I realized that my main reason for doing so was very simple. I needed a vegan cookery book myself. At last, instead of combing endless cookery books, vegetarian and otherwise, for vegan recipes, I could accumulate all my favourite recipes inside one cover. I hope also to meet the needs of, at least three different groups of people.

I have written firstly for those who, like myself, have adopted a vegan diet on principle. We feel that not only does meat production involve unnecessary suffering and death, but so do dairy farming and egg production. We abhor the fact that hens are confined in battery cages to deliver an endless stream of eggs for human consumption. We feel appalled that calves are torn from their mothers and possibly reared in the darkened crates of modern veal units, so that humans can drink their mothers' milk. So we abstain from eggs and dairy foods as well as meat. But, rather than adopt a negative attitude, I expect most of us like to show our friends and work-mates that we can live not only in good health, but also in culinary comfort, on a vegan diet. We know that no parliamentary decree will ban the horrors of factory farming. We just hope that individuals can start a chain reaction of compassion throughout society, so that one day the demand for meat, milk and eggs will fade away, and our domestic animals can be liberated. This liberation is basic to a New Age.

I have written also for the many thousands of you who have already adopted a vegetarian diet, would like to be vegan, but wonder how you can make the change. I sympathize — I too was a vegetarian for four years before I felt I could cope with the next step. As it turns out I have had no regrets, and hope that the change-over can perhaps be facilitated for you by this book of vegan recipes.

But I feel sure there is another group of people who will welcome this book. I refer to those of you who wish to cut down your intake of animal flesh and fats for health reasons. Many of you will have read articles in newspapers and magazines hinting at a possible link between flesh-eating and some forms of cancer. Others will know that saturated animal fats are considered by many to be a contributary factory in coronary disease. Others will have been advised by their doctors to adopt a vegan diet (and will be wondering where to begin). I sincerely hope you will enjoy the recipes in this book. For you, and for all the people who have so often said to me, 'But what *do* you eat?' I have written this book.

Soups

For the soup-maker new to veganism the main problem is flavour, as beef and chicken stock are no longer used. There is no need to worry. Apart from the excellent vegetable stock cubes available in healthfood shops and high-class grocers, it is very easy to maintain a supply of home-made vegetable stock. Keep all water in which vegetables have been cooked — even potato water. Don't throw away vegetable peelings. Wash the vegetables before peeling and when you have a good supply of, for example, potato, carrot, leek or celery peelings boil them for twenty minutes or so in a large saucepan, strain the stock and keep it in the fridge. The stock will taste even better if you fry the peelings in a little margarine before adding the water.

Most vegetable soups can have their flavour enhanced by the

addition of all or any of the following: yeast extract, lemon juice, tomato purée, soy sauce and black pepper. Left-over cooked beans and lentils can be added whole to many soups, or mashed or liquidized to a purée and then added. Larger quantities of left-over beans can be liquidized with stock or water until of a soup-like consistency, then flavoured with any of the suitable flavourings already mentioned to make a nourishing soup.

Many of the soups in this section can act as meals in themselves, if served with wholemeal bread, and followed by fresh fruit or a fruit pudding.

BORTSCH

1 bunch young beetroot
2 onions
1 oz (30 g) margarine
2 pints (1 litre) water or
  stock

1 lemon
1 teaspoon yeast extract
1 teaspoon brown sugar
salt
parsley

Chop the onions and fry gently in the margarine. Do not brown them. Add the beetroot, which you have washed and shredded. Pour in water or stock and the juice of the lemon, add yeast extract, sugar and salt to taste. Simmer for about 40 minutes. Mash slightly or whizz in your liquidizer for a few seconds.

Reheat, and serve garnished with chopped parsley.

CHILLED CUCUMBER AND MINT SOUP

3 cucumbers
1 bunch spring onions
3 tablespoons chopped
  fresh mint

1 tablespoon soya flour
2 pints (1 litre) stock
salt and black pepper

Reserve a little cucumber cut in strips and chilled. Peel and slice cucumbers and onions and place in pan with stock. Bring to the boil and simmer until tender. Sieve or liquidize with soya flour. Return to pan and bring to boil. Season and add mint.

Chill and serve garnished with cucumber strips.

CREAMED LEEK AND POTATO SOUP

1 lb (450g) leeks
1 lb (450g) potatoes
2 tablespoons soya flour
2 oz (60g) margarine
2 pints (1 litre)
  water

salt and black pepper
a few leaves fresh sage
parsley
chives

Peel leeks, wash well and slice, discarding only the toughest green parts. Peel potatoes and cut in chunks. Melt margarine and fry leeks gently for a few minutes. Add potatoes, stir, then pour in the water. Season, bring to the boil and simmer until the vegetables are tender. Cool slightly and then liquidize, adding soya flour.

Return to rinsed pan, add chopped sage and parsley and check seasoning. Bring to the boil and serve garnished with chopped chives.

CREAM OF MUSHROOM SOUP

8 oz (230g) fresh
  mushrooms
1 onion
1 clove garlic (optional)
2 oz (60g) margarine
1½ pints (850ml) stock

½ pint (300ml) Plamil or
Granogen, reconstituted
  (see p. 132–3)
1 teaspoon yeast extract
salt and black pepper
parsley

Peel and chop onion and garlic, and fry gently in margarine for a few minutes. Add finely chopped mushrooms. Stir in flour and slowly add stock. Bring to the boil and simmer for about 10 minutes, stirring occasionally. Add Plamil, yeast extract and seasoning.

Reheat, check flavour and serve garnished with parsley.

CREME DE PROVENCE

1 lb (450g) tomatoes
1 lb (450g) potatoes
1 large onion
4 oz (100g) button onions
½ oz (15g) margarine

2 cloves garlic
a little thyme or basil
salt
black pepper
parsley

Skin the tomatoes, peel and chop the potatoes, chop the onion and garlic finely. Place all in large pan with thyme, seasoning and water or stock to cover. Bring to the boil, cover and simmer very gently for 2 hours. Pour off the liquid, sieve or liquidize the vegetables and return them to the rinsed pan with enough of their liquid to make a thick but runny soup.

Peel the button onions and boil in salted water until tender, about 10 minutes. Add them to the soup, bring it to the boil and add the margarine and chopped parsley just before serving.

Remember to keep the onion water and any excess soup liquid for your stockpot.

GARLIC SOUP

12 cloves of garlic
sprigs of thyme, rosemary
  and bay leaves

salt and black pepper
2 pints (1 litre) water
3 tablespoons olive oil

Boil the water, add the peeled garlic cloves and herbs. Simmer for 15 minutes, then stir in the oil to thicken, and simmer for 10 minutes more. Season. Serve with slices of hot brown toast.

This is an old French recipe and is supposed to do wonders for your health. In fact the French call it the Soup of Life.

GAZPACHO

1 onion
1 small cucumber
1 green pepper
4 tomatoes
2 cloves of garlic
2 large slices of bread
2 tablespoons lemon juice

4 tablespoons olive oil
1 tin tomato juice (or
  tomato purée with
  water)
1 teaspoon brown sugar
salt and black pepper
watercress or parsley

Remove crusts from bread and soak it in some of the tomato juice. Add crushed garlic, lemon juice, oil and seasoning. Mix well and stir in grated cucumber, finely chopped pepper and onion. Skin the tomatoes and sieve to remove pips. Add the tomatoes and rest of juice. Mash everything well.

Check seasoning and add more water if too thick. Chill and serve garnished with watercress or parsley.

This soup can be made very quickly in a liquidizer. Liquidize all the ingredients, and then add the oil slowly. Check seasoning and consistency as before.

GREEN PEA SOUP

1 lb (450g) fresh peas
a few spring onions
1 teaspoon salt
1 teaspoon brown sugar

2 tablespoons soya flour
1 oz (30g) margarine
2 pints (1 litre) stock
fresh mint or sage

Clean and chop onions, and fry them gently in the margarine for a minute. Add shelled peas, stock and seasoning. Bring to the boil and simmer for 20 minutes. Liquidize or mash with the soya flour. Return to the rinsed pan and reheat to boiling point.

Check seasoning and consistency. Serve garnished with fresh chopped mint or sage.

If the peas are really young and fresh, you can boil the washed pods with the soup, or use them to flavour the stock before you make the soup.

GUACAMOLE SOUP

1 avocado pear
1 small onion
1 clove of garlic
1 tablespoon lemon juice

1 large tin tomato juice
salt and black pepper
parsley

Peel and crush garlic with salt. Mash the avocado and add the onion, grated, the lemon juice and garlic. Mix in the tomato juice, season and chill. Serve garnished with chopped parsley.

HEARTY VEGETABLE SOUP

1 onion
1 turnip
2-3 carrots
1-2 leeks
½ green pepper
2 oz (60g) fresh or frozen
  peas

2 tomatoes
2 oz (60g) margarine
2 pints (1 litre) stock or
  water
2 tablespoons semolina or
  cornmeal
2 bay leaves

1 teaspoon yeast extract

1 teaspoon soy sauce

salt and black pepper

parsley

Peel first four vegetables, and cut into small pieces. Remove seeds and stalk from pepper and cut in strips. Shell peas and skin and chop tomatoes. Melt margarine and fry all vegetables for a few minutes, until they are well coated with fat. Add stock or water and bayleaves and simmer until vegetables are nearly cooked. (If using frozen peas add them now.) Sprinkle over semolina or cornmeal, stirring well.

Simmer for another 30 minutes, add seasonings, and serve garnished with chopped parsley.

LENTIL SOUP

6 oz (180g) red lentils

1 onion

2 pints (1 litre) stock or
 water

1 tablespoon tomato purée

1 teaspoon yeast extract

1 tablespoon lemon juice

salt and black pepper

parsley

Clean and wash lentils. Place them in a large pan with the water or stock, the onion, peeled, and a good teaspoon of salt. Bring to the boil and simmer until very soft, about 20 minutes. Cool slightly, remove onion if liked, and sieve or liquidize. Return to rinsed pan, adding more water if necessary to get the consistency you like.

Reheat and season with tomato purée, yeast extract, lemon juice and black pepper. Check salt seasoning. Serve garnished with chopped parsley.

MINESTRONE

2 potatoes

3 carrots

1 onion

2 cloves of garlic

4 tomatoes

3 oz (90g) cooked peas or
 kidney beans

1 oz (30g) spaghetti

2 pints (1 litre) stock or
 water

3 tablespoons olive oil

2 teaspoons herbs,
 preferably basil, sage,
 oregano

salt and black pepper

Peel and chop potatoes, scrape and slice carrots, wash and slice tomatoes, removing skins first if preferred. Heat oil, add chopped onion and garlic, potatoes and carrots, and fry gently for a few minutes.

Add the stock or water and herbs. Bring to the boil and simmer for 15 minutes. Add peas or beans and tomatoes, and simmer for another 15 minutes.

Add spaghetti, broken into small pieces, and season. Simmer until spaghetti is just tender. Check seasoning and serve garnished with parsley.

MULLIGATAWNY SOUP

2 onions
1 clove of garlic
2 carrots
1 cooking apple
3 oz (90g) cooked lentils or
　white beans
2 pints (1 litre) stock
2 bay leaves

2 tablespoons vegetable oil
1 tablespoon garam masala or curry powder
1 tablespoon lemon juice
salt and black pepper
fresh coriander leaves or parsley

Peel and chop onion and garlic, and fry in oil until starting to brown. Add garam masala and finely chopped carrot and apple. Mash or liquidize beans and stir in. Pour in stock, add seasoning and bay leaves. Bring to the boil and simmer for 20 minutes.

Add lemon juice and check seasoning, adding a little more garam masala or black pepper before serving. Garnish with chopped coriander leaves or parsley.

NETTLE SOUP

1 large onion
1-2 lb (450-900g) young
　nettles
2 pints (1 litre) water

2 tablespoons olive oil
2 tablespoons soya flour
1 clove of garlic (optional)
salt and black pepper

Peel and chop onion and garlic, and fry gently in oil for a few minutes. Add washed and chopped nettles, and stir with wooden spoon for a few minutes more. Add the water and seasoning. Bring to the boil and simmer for 15 minutes.

Cool slightly and liquidize or sieve with soya flour. Bring back to the boil in rinsed pan, check seasoning and serve garnished with chopped fresh sage or parsley.

This soup may be made using the green tops of red radishes instead of nettles.

QUICK MISO SOUP

2 tablespoons Miso (see
  p. 133)
1 tablespoon tomato purée
1 tablespoon lemon juice
1 teaspoon Tamari soy
  sauce

2 pints (1 litre) water
1 teaspoon yeast extract
salt and black pepper

Place Miso in pan with tomato purée. Add water gradually, stirring well. Bring to the boil, simmer 2 minutes, adding the rest of the ingredients. Go easy on the salt; you may not need any.

Serve with crisp croûtons of fried bread on top, or with slices of wholemeal bread.

To make a more substantial soup, thicken with left-over beans or lentils puréed, or add 2 tablespoons semolina or cornmeal and simmer for 30 minutes. You may need to add a little more water if using the last method.

QUICK VEGETABLE SOUP
(liquidizer required)

2 large potatoes
a variety of vegetables,
  e.g. carrot, turnip,
  tomato, greens,
  cauliflower
1 large onion
1 oz (30g) margarine

2 pints (1 litre) stock or
  water
1 teaspoon yeast extract
1 teaspoon soy sauce
a little lemon juice
salt and black pepper

Peel and chop onion and fry in margarine until turning brown. Meanwhile clean vegetables and chop roughly. Put them in liquidizer with some of the liquid. Liquidize until a purée. Add to onion with rest of stock or water, bring to the boil, stirring occasionally, and simmer for about 15 minutes. Season and serve.

SPINACH SOUP

1 lb (450g) spinach
1 clove of garlic (optional)
2 pints (1 litre) stock or
  water
2 oz (60g) margarine

2 tablespoons cornmeal
  flour or semolina
1 oz (30g) flour
a little grated nutmeg
salt and pepper

Melt margarine, stir in flour. Add washed spinach and gradually add the water or stock. Season, bring to the boil, then sprinkle on the cornmeal, stirring well. Simmer for 30 minutes, stirring occasionally.

Cool slightly, liquidize or sieve, and reheat. Serve garnished with chopped mint.

SPRING VEGETABLE SOUP

1 bunch spring onions
about 6 small new carrots
3 oz (90g) young runner or
  French beans
2 oz (60g) fresh peas

1 small green pepper
6 small new potatoes
1½ pints (850ml) stock
1 teaspoon yeast extract
salt and black pepper

Shell peas. Chop other vegetables finely, unless you have a liquidizer. If you have, just place vegetables and a little water in liquidizer and whizz for a few seconds, until the vegetables are finely chopped. Bring the stock to the boil, add peas, then rest of vegetables.

Season and simmer for a few minutes, until vegetables are tender.

Check seasoning and serve garnished with chopped chives.

TOMATO SOUP

1½ lb (670g) tomatoes
1 onion
1 clove of garlic
2 tablespoons soya flour
2 pints (1 litre) stock, or 1
  pint (500ml) stock, 1
  pint (500ml) soya milk

2 tablespoons olive oil
2 bay leaves
1 teaspoon brown sugar
salt and black pepper
fresh parsley, marjoram
  or basil

Peel and chop onion and garlic and fry gently in oil. Add washed and chopped tomatoes and continue to fry gently for a few minutes. Add bay leaves, seasoning and stock. If using soya milk do not add it yet. Simmer for a few minutes, cool slightly and liquidize or sieve, adding soya flour. Return to rinsed pan, adding milk if you are using it, bring to the boil.

Check seasoning, and serve garnished with the fresh, chopped herb.

WATERCRESS SOUP

1 onion
2 potatoes
1 bunch watercress
1½ (850ml) pints stock or
   water

1 oz (30g) margarine
2 tablespoons soya flour
salt and black pepper

Fry chopped onion in margarine for a few minutes and add the peeled and chopped potato. Stir well and add the stock or water, the well-washed watercress and seasoning. Bring to the boil and simmer for 10 minutes. Cool slightly and mash well or liquidize with the soya flour.

Reheat to boiling point, check seasoning, and serve hot or chilled.

Starters and Snacks

Your choice of starter dish will depend on the main course to follow. Something cool and slippery like Marinated Mushrooms goes well before a heavy main course. A more substantial starter such as Chilled Nut Savoury will combine with a lighter vegetable dish to follow

Snacks such as Vegan Rarebit or Pakoras can often take the place of one of the day's meals, if eaten with fresh fruit or a salad.

Those of you who eat a packed lunch will enjoy experimenting with new flavours added to the basic Sandwich Spread. You will also find that Samosas and Sosmix Rolls make a pleasant change from sandwiches, and are equally delicious eaten cold.

AUBERGINE PATE

1 lb (450g) aubergines
2 tablespoons olive oil
1 oz (30g) margarine
3 tablespoons lemon juice

a few stoned black olives
salt and black pepper
crisp lettuce heart or
  cucumber and tomato

Halve aubergines, sprinkle cut surfaces with salt and leave for 30 minutes. Dry surfaces, brush with a little oil and bake in a slow oven until flesh is black. Cool, scoop out flesh and mash it with the margarine, oil, lemon juice and seasoning. Chop the olives and stir them in.

Chill well, and serve garnished with the fresh salad vegetables. Thin slices of hot toast go well with this dish.

AVOCADO SURPRISE

3 avocado pears
1 green pepper
1 small chilli pepper
1 tomato

2 tablespoons French
  dressing
salt and black pepper

Skin the tomato and remove the seeds (to stockpot) and mash it with the finely chopped pepper and chilli. Use your liquidizer to do this if you have one. Halve and stone the pears, scoop out flesh and add to the other vegetables. Mash well and moisten with the dressing. Fill 4 half shells with this mixture and cover with foil until serving time. Serve with spring onions and lettuce.

Try to make this dish as close to serving time as possible.

CHANNA

6 oz (180g) channa dahl
  (split yellow peas)
1 teaspoon garam masala

$\frac{1}{4}$ teaspoon chilli powder
1 teaspoon salt
oil or ghee to fry

Pour 2 pints of boiling water onto the washed channa and leave overnight. Drain and dry the channa. Heat the oil and fry the channa dahl, a little at a time. Mix it well with the spices and salt. This makes a good appetizer. The mixture will keep well in an airtight container.

CHILLED NUT SAVOURY

4 oz (120g) ground nuts,
  e.g. cashews, walnuts
3 oz (90g) breadcrumbs
3 spring onions or 1 small
  onion

1 large tomato
1 tablespoon olive oil
parsley
salt and black pepper

This dish is really easy to make if you have a liquidizer, as you can grind your own nuts and make your breadcrumbs quickly. You can then liquidize the tomato, onions and oil together and add them to the dry ingredients.

Otherwise sieve the tomato, and mix with the oil and grated onions, then add to the dry mixture. Season carefully, and stir in some chopped parsley. Press the mixture into a greased bowl and chill it. Turn out to serve and sprinkle more parsley on top.

Although this makes a nutritious starter to a meal, a greater quantity can be served as a main dish with a salad on summer days.

CHURA

8 oz (230g) Rice Krispies
  or puffed rice
3 oz (90g) peanuts
3 oz (90g) cashew nuts
2 oz (60g) raisins
2 oz (60g) grated coconut
  (optional)

$\frac{1}{2}$ teaspoon turmeric
  powder
$\frac{1}{2}$ teaspoon cumin powder
$\frac{1}{2}$ teaspoon paprika
$\frac{1}{4}$ teaspoon chilli powder
1 teaspoon salt
oil or ghee for frying

Heat oil and fry turmeric and cumin. Add nuts and raisins and fry for a few minutes. Stir in coconut rice, salt, paprika and chilli.

This makes a delicious between-meals nibble. The mixture will keep well if stored in an airtight container.

GARLIC MUSHROOMS

1 lb (450g) button
  mushrooms
3 cloves of garlic

3 oz (90g) margarine
salt and black pepper
fresh chives or parsley

Wipe mushrooms clean and cook gently in melted margarine with pressed or crushed garlic for about 5 minutes. Season and cool.

Serve garnished with chopped chives or parsley, and accompanied by fresh brown bread.

HERBED LOAF

3-4 oz (1000g) margarine
1 loaf French bread
2 cloves of garlic
1 tablespoon finely
   chopped dried parsley

$\frac{1}{4}$ teaspoon thyme
$\frac{1}{2}$ teaspoon marjoram
   powder
$\frac{1}{2}$ teaspoon black pepper

Peel and crush the garlic, and work it into the margarine with the herbs and pepper. Cut the bread in slices down to, but not through, the bottom crust. Spread one side of each slice with the mixture, wrap it in foil and bake it at about 325°F — Mark 3 for 15 minutes. Serve at once, with hot soup, salata or a dip.

HUMUS

6 oz (180g) chick peas,
   cooked (see p. 27)
5 tablespoons Tahini
   (sesame spread)
2 tablespoons olive oil

5 tablespoons lemon juice
2 cloves of garlic
salt and black pepper
parsley

Sieve chick peas, or whizz them in your liquidizer until they are a purée. Put the garlic through a press or crush it finely. Mix all the ingredients except the parsley, which can be chopped and used as a garnish. Serve with crisp lettuce and cucumber, or thin it with some bean liquid or lemon juice and serve as a dip, with crisps, celery stalks and crispbread.

JELLIED MELON AND MINT

4 tablespoons lemon juice
$\frac{1}{4}$ oz (10g) agar-agar (see
   p. 94)

1 tablespoon sugar
1 teaspoon mint sauce
1 small Honeydew melon

Make juice up to $\frac{3}{4}$ pint with water, bring to boil, and sprinkle on agar-agar, stirring well. Cool, then stir in finely ground sugar and mint sauce. Cube the melon flesh and stir into the nearly set jelly. Serve in individual glasses, chilled.

LENTIL FRITTERS

8 oz (230g) lentils
3 onions
2 tomatoes
1 thick slice wholemeal
  bread, crumbed
2 oz (60g) margarine

1 level tablespoon curry
  powder
salt
oil to fry
parsley

Wash lentils and cook with salt in as little water as possible. Meanwhile melt the margarine, add the curry powder, finely chopped onions and tomatoes, and cook until the mixture is thick. Add to cooked lentils and stir in breadcrumbs to give a thick consistency. Heat the oil and fry spoonfuls of the mixture until light brown on both sides.

Garnish with chopped parsley and serve with chutney and salad.

MARINATED MUSHROOMS

1 lb (450g) button
  mushrooms
3 oz (90g) margarine
4 spring onions or 1 onion
2 tablespoons lemon juice
2 cloves of garlic
2 bay leaves

1 teaspoon brown sugar
salt and black pepper
1 glass white wine (or
  stock)
$\frac{1}{2}$ teaspoon marjoram
parsley

Chop onions and fry gently in margarine for a few minutes. Add cleaned mushrooms, juice, seasoning, bay leaves and marjoram. Cook gently until the watery liquid has evaporated, about 15 minutes. Now add the crushed garlic and wine (or stock), bring to the boil and cool. Stir in about a tablespoonful of chopped parsley and check the seasoning.

Leave for several hours before serving garnished with chopped parsley. This dish is good served with fresh brown bread.

MUSHROOM AND TOMATO SNACK

8 oz (230g) mushrooms
8 oz (230g) tomatoes
2 oz (60g) margarine
1 tablespoon flour
½ pint (300ml) stock
1 teaspoon soy sauce

salt and black pepper
a few bean sprouts
1 tablespoon wheatgerm
(optional)
parsley
4 slices wholemeal bread

Melt margarine and fry cleaned, halved mushrooms for 2 minutes. Add washed, quartered tomatoes, and continue to cook until juice runs. Stir in flour and add stock slowly. Boil for 2 minutes, stirring and then add seasoning, bean sprouts and wheatgerm.

Serve on the toasted bread, garnished with chopped parsley.

MUSHROOM CRUNCH

8 oz (230g) button
   mushrooms
4 stalks celery

6-8 stoned black olives
about 5 tablespoons
   French dressing (see
   p. 92)

Wash and dice the celery and leave it to soak in cold salted water to crisp it. Wipe the mushrooms clean, and chop the olives. Just before serving, mix all the ingredients together, moistening with the dressing.

Serve with crispbread or thin toast.

MUSHROOM PATTIES

8 oz (230g) Rough-Puff
   pastry (see recipe for
   Sosmix Rolls, p. 23)
2 oz (60g) margarine
1½ oz (50g) flour

up to ½ pint (300ml) soya
   or plant milk (see p. 132–3)
8 oz (230g) mushrooms
salt and black pepper
parsley

Make the pastry first. Turn the oven on to 425°F — Mark 7 and make the filling, while the pastry cools in the fridge.

Melt the margarine, add the cleaned, chopped mushrooms and cook gently for a few minutes. Stir in the flour, then (off the flame) slowly stir in enough milk to give a very thick sauce. Boil for 2 minutes, stirring all the time. Add seasoning and some chopped parsley. Cover and leave to cool.

Roll out pastry and cut into 3-inch rounds. Use a 1-inch cutter to remove the centres from half of the rounds. Put the uncut rounds on the baking sheet, brush with soya milk, and place the 3-inch rounds without centres on top, pressing down well. Now place the small circles on top. Leave for a few minutes, then bake for about 20 minutes. Remove from baking sheet, cool, remove small circles, fill and replace circles.

Serve cold, or reheat for a few minutes at 325°F — Mark 3.

NUT PATÉ

3 oz (90g) Cashewnutta or
  Nutter (nut butter)
2 oz (60g) ground almonds
1 oz (30g) roasted,
  chopped almonds
4 stoned black olives

1 large tin Tartex
  (vegetarian pâté)
salt and black pepper
watercress, endive or
  lettuce

Soften the nut butter and stir in the ground and chopped almonds. Combine with the Tartex, season and add 2 of the olives, chopped finely. Serve from small dish, garnished with remaining olives, and surrounded by salad greens.

OATCAKES

6 oz (180g) rolled oats
1 onion
2 tomatoes
2 tablespoons tomato purée
1 teaspoon soy sauce

pinch dried sage
1 tablespoon gram flour
  (see p. 132)
3 fl. oz (100ml) oil
salt and black pepper

Mix the tomato purée and soy sauce. Stir in the oats and seasoning. Add enough water to make a fairly firm mixture, then allow this mixture to stand while chopping the onion and tomatoes into very fine pieces. Add them to the mixture with the sifted gram flour. Add more water if the mixture is too stiff. Heat the oil, drop in spoonfuls of the oat mixture and fry until browned on both sides.

This dish goes with Potatoes and Mushrooms (p. 76) and a green salad.

PAKORAS

8 oz (230g) gram flour (see
  p. 132)
2 teaspoons baking
  powder
2 teaspoons garam masala
2 green chillies, or
  ½ teaspoon chilli powder

1 teaspoon salt
2 onions
1 carrot
1 potato
plenty of oil or vegetable
  ghee for frying

Sieve flour, baking powder and salt into a large bowl. Add garam masala, then add enough cold water to make a fairly thick paste. Chop the chillies and vegetables very finely and stir in. Heat the oil and drop spoonfuls of the mixture into it and fry until light brown on all sides. Fry fairly slowly, so that all the vegetables become tender.

These are delicious served with chutney.

PASTA STARTER

3 oz (90g) spaghetti rings
1 tablespoon Smokey Snaps
1 crisp eating apple
1 small onion

6 tablespoons French dressir
1 teaspoon concentrated
  curry sauce (or curry
  powder and water)
parsley

Cook spaghetti until just tender, drain and rinse. Chop onion and apple, mix with Smokey Snaps, sauce and dressing. Fold gently into the spaghetti and serve cold, garnished with chopped parsley.

SALATA

1 large onion
1 large carrot
1 green pepper
1 red pepper
8 oz (230g) tomatoes
1 clove of garlic

3 tablespoons olive oil
1 tablespoon lemon juice
  or wine vinegar
salt and black pepper
parsley

Peel and slice onion. Cut carrot in thin strips and fry gently with onion in oil for a few minutes. Add peppers, cut in long strips and cook for a few more minutes. Skin and slice the tomatoes, crush the garlic and add to pan. Cover pan and continue to cook gently until carrot is tender, stirring from time to time. Season well and add juice.

Chill and serve garnished with chopped parsley. This dish is good with toast or fresh wholemeal bread.

SAMOSAS

1 lb (450g) 81% self-raising flour
1 oz (30g) melted margarine or ghee
1 teaspoon salt

Filling:
2 oz (60g) margarine or ghee
1 lb (450g) boiled potatoes

1 onion
2 tablespoons cooked peas
2 green chillies or ½ teaspoon chilli powder
1 teaspoon garam masala
a few fresh coriander or parsley leaves
salt
plenty of ghee or oil to fry

Sieve flour and salt into bowl, add margarine, mix and add enough water to bind. Knead well and leave to stand, covered with a damp cloth.

For the filling, melt the fat and fry the chopped onion for a few minutes. Add the diced potatoes, peas, chillies, coriander and garam masala and salt. Fry for 5 minutes more and leave to cool.

Knead dough again. Make small balls of it and roll each ball out thinly on floured board until saucer-sized. Cut each circle in half, put some filling on one half and place the other half on top. Press the edges down to seal, moistening with water if necessary. When all the samosas are ready, fry them in oil until crisp and golden.

Serve with chutney and salad.

SANDWICH SPREAD

8 oz (230g) margarine
2 oz (60g) soya flour (must be a heat-treated brand)

2 tablespoons boiling water

Cream the margarine, mix in the flour and add the water slowly, beating well. To this basic spread you can add, per 2 oz spread:

3 teaspoons curry powder
1 teaspoon yeast extract
2 teaspoons lemon juice

or:
2 oz (60g) chopped, salted
    nuts
1 tablespoon Tahini
1 teaspoon soy sauce

or:
1 tablespoon tomato purée
1 tablespoon Tahini

or:
2 tablespoons chopped
    fresh herbs
1 teaspoon lemon juice
black pepper
1 crushed clove of garlic
    (optional)

SCOTCH TOMATOES

4 very large or 8 medium
    tomatoes
about ½ packet Sosmix (see
    p. 133) or a rissole mix

2 oz (60g) margarine
parsley

Make up mix with cold water as directed. Flatten it out and roll each tomato in a coating of mix, sealing the edges with water. Melt margarine in an ovenproof dish, roll the tomatoes in this, then bake at 400°F — Mark 6 for 30 minutes, basting once.

Serve hot with green salad, and garnished with parsley.

SIMPLE AVOCADO STARTER

2 ripe avocado pears
French dressing

crisp lettuce leaves

Halve avocados, removing stones. Allow half an avocado per person. Just before serving fill the hollows left by the stones with French dressing. Surround with lettuce leaves.

SOSMIX ROLLS

½ packet Sosmix (see
   p. 133), mixed with
   water as directed

Rough-Puff Pastry:
8 oz (230g) strong brown flour

6 oz (180g) margarine
1 teaspoon salt
¼ pint (150ml) of ice-cold
   water
1 tablespoon lemon juice

Sieve flour and salt into bowl. Add margarine in small pieces. Add juice and enough water to bind into an elastic dough. Place on floured board and roll away from yourself into a long strip. Flour lightly, damp edges with water, fold in three, give it a half turn and roll again. Repeat 4 times to mix fat evenly. Leave to cool in fridge for 20 minutes and turn on your oven to 425°F — Mark 7.

Roll out pastry ¼-inch thick, cut into rectangles and place a roll of Sosmix on each one. Fold the pastry over and seal edges with water. Placing seal underneath, make a few slits on the top of each roll. Place on greased baking sheet and bake for about 25 minutes, or until a light brown on top.

TOMATO DIP

2 tablespoons olive oil
1½ lb (670g) tomatoes
2 onions
1 clove of garlic
1 small green pepper

1 teaspoon brown sugar
2 bay leaves
½ teaspoon marjoram
salt and black pepper
good dash of Tabasco
   sauce

Peel and grate onion and crush garlic. Fry both gently in oil. Add pepper, very finely chopped, and cook for 2 minutes more. Add skinned, chopped tomatoes, herbs and seasoning. Simmer uncovered for 15 minutes until thickened. Add dash of Tabasco, and check seasoning. Serve in individual bowls, surrounded by cubes of brown bread to dip into mixture with forks.

VEGAN KEBAB

1 green pepper
4 oz (120g) mushrooms
2 tomatoes
1 oz (30g) large, seedless
  raisins

4 oz (120g) stoned dates
2 tablespoons soya sauce
1 tablespoon lemon juice
1 tablespoon olive oil
seasoning to taste

Clean vegetables. Halve large mushrooms and cut pepper into 1-inch squares. Combine liquids and seasoning in a shallow dish and add all the ingredients except the tomatoes. Leave for a couple of hours, stirring occasionally. Add the cubed tomatoes, then stick all the ingredients on 4 skewers.

Place a sheet of foil on the grill-pan and place skewers on it, keeping handles clear of heat. Grill for about 7 minutes, basting and turning occasionally. Serve at once, with the remaining marinade in a separate dish. This can be eaten as a starter or with rice and curry.

VEGAN RAREBIT

4 slices wholemeal bread
2 oz (60g) margarine
4 tablespoons tomato
  purée

4 tablespoons Tahini
2 teaspoons soy sauce
black pepper

Melt margarine, stir in other ingredients, heat through and serve on the toasted bread.

Main Courses

I have arranged the main course dishes in four basic groups: Beans and Pulses, Nuts, Textured Vegetable Protein and Vegetables. I have added sections on pasta and cereal dishes, though in fact many of the main dishes are best served with a cereal accompaniment, which not only tastes good but also adds to the protein content of the meal. Many of the ingredients in the dishes are suggested, rather than compulsory. Feel free to use substitutes or to add your favourite vegetable or herb, or to vary the amount and type of seasoning used. With skill, and perhaps luck, you will be able to serve the same basic dish twice, and no-one will even notice!

Beans, nuts and T.V.P. are all worth buying in bulk if you can. Prices do vary from shop to shop, so it is worth doing a little detective work before spending your money. If you live far from a major town it is also worth pestering your local 'class' grocer. With a little persuasion you may soon have him stocking all sorts of beans and health food products he never dreamed of before. If you have friends nearby who are interested in health food, it could also be worth your while to share the costs of a monthly expedition to your nearest bulk-buy health food shop. Vegetable cooking oil varies tremendously in price and is definitely worth buying by the gallon. If you have an Indian food store near you they will probably stock it cheaply, and will also have a wide range of spices and pulses.

By varying the basic type of dish, you should meet all your body's protein requirements. It is sensible to keep a supply of nuts in the kitchen for between-meals nibbles. Vitamin B12 is the only vitamin which could be lacking in a vegan diet. However it is an ingredient of Granogen soya milk, Plamil plant milk and Barmene yeast extract. Some people can synthesize B12 naturally in their intestines, but anyone worried about nutritional deficiency can also take a B12 tablet daily. Vitamin D can be provided, not only by sunshine, but by using Tomor margarine, which is fortified with this vitamin. Children should be encouraged to drink a pint of Plamil or Granogen milk every day. This can be taken partly in cooking — sauces, custards, etc. These milks can also be used to make traditional favourites such as cocoa, milk shake, etc.

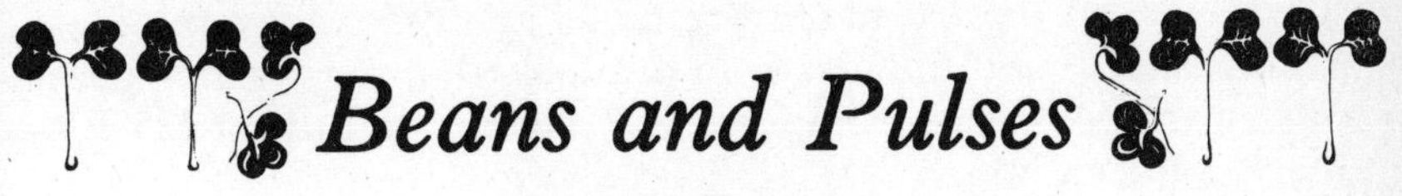

Beans and Pulses

BAKED BEANS

12 oz (340g) haricot beans
1 onion
1 clove of garlic
2 sticks of celery
2 carrots
4 tomatoes

1 tablespoon tomato purée
2 teaspoons paprika
1 teaspoon brown sugar
salt
4 tablespoons oil

Soak the beans overnight or pour boiling water over them and leave them for an hour. Then boil them until nearly tender, or cook under pressure for 6 minutes. Peel and chop the vegetables and fry gently in the oil for 10 minutes. Liquidize or sieve this mixture.

Place the beans in an ovenproof dish and stir in the puréed vegetables, tomato purée, paprika and seasonings. Add a little of the bean liquid or stock so that the beans are just covered. Cover and cook at 250°F — Mark 1 for an hour or until beans are fully tender.

Try serving this dish with Chappatis (p. 59) and Stir-Fry Spinach (p. 79), or boiled rice and a green salad.

BAKED CHICK PEAS

8 oz (230g) chick peas
4 tomatoes
2 onions
1 green pepper
2 cloves of garlic
½ teaspoon marjoram

pinch sage
1 tablespoon chopped
 parsley
1 tablespoon lemon juice
3 tablespoons olive oil
salt and black pepper

Soak the chick peas overnight or pour boiling water over them and leave for an hour. Boil them gently until just tender, or cook them under pressure for about 20 minutes. Skin and quarter the tomatoes, slice the pepper and onion and crush the garlic.

Heat the oil and fry all the vegetables gently for a few minutes. Add the herbs and finally stir in the cooked, drained chick peas. Season and cook in an ovenproof dish, covered tightly, at 325°F— Mark 3 for an hour.

Try serving hot with creamed spinach and pan-fried potatoes, or cold with Salad Niçoise.

BAKED LENTILS

12 oz (350g) red lentils
2 onions
2 cloves of garlic
3 slices wholemeal bread
2 tablespoons chopped
  parsley
3 tablespoons lemon juice

1 tablespoon soy sauce
1 teaspoon yeast extract
2 tablespoons oil
2 teaspoons freshly
  ground black pepper
salt

Wash the lentils and cook in plenty of water for about 20 minutes until tender. Peel and chop the onion and garlic and fry gently in the oil for 10 minutes. Make breadcrumbs and add to the onions with the parsley. Add all the other ingredients, then add the mashed or liquidized lentils. Cook gently for a few minutes, checking seasoning and adding more water if too stiff. The mixture should be fairly thick. Turn into a greased overproof dish and cook at 350°F — Mark 4 for 30 minutes.

This dish can be served cold with a tomato salad and a green salad or hot with Beans and Almonds (p. 66) and Stuffed Tomatoes (p. 81).

BEAN AND VEGETABLE STEW

4 oz (120g) butter beans
2 oz (60g) lentils
3 onions
3 carrots
3 tomatoes
1 green pepper
1 turnip

2 sticks celery
2 bay leaves
1 teaspoon yeast extract
1 tablespoon soy sauce
1 tablespoon lemon juice
salt and black pepper

Soak the beans overnight or pour boiling water over them and leave for an hour. Simmer them in about 2 pints liquid until half-cooked. Add the washed lentils and continue simmering for about 30 minutes. Now add the bay leaves and sliced vegetables, allowing more time for the root vegetables. When everything is tender, add the soy sauce, juice, yeast extract and seasoning.

Serve with freshly-baked wholemeal bread or Chappatis (p. 59).

BEAN HOT-POT

6 oz (180g) haricot or fava beans	3 tablespoons tomato purée
2 onions	1 tablespoon soy sauce
2 carrots	1 teaspoon yeast extract
3 tomatoes	1 pint (550ml) stock
2 oz (60g) mushrooms	salt and black pepper
3 large potatoes	2 bay leaves
2 oz (60g) margarine	

Soak beans overnight, or cover with boiling water and leave for an hour. Fry the chopped onions in the margarine until starting to brown, then place them in the bottom of a greased ovenproof dish. Cover with the sliced tomatoes, the soaked beans, the sliced carrots and mushrooms. Place the sliced potatoes on top.

Pour the stock into the onion pan, and bring to the boil with the tomato purée, soy sauce, yeast extract, bay leaves and seasoning. Pour it carefully over the vegetables in the dish, cover and cook at 300°F — Mark 2 for 2½ hours. Remove lid for last 15 minutes, and check that beans are tender before serving.

Try serving with boiled buckwheat and salad.

BLACK-EYED BEAN CURRY

8 oz (230g) black-eyed beans	1 teaspoon minced ginger or ½ teaspoon ginger powder
2 onions	
1 clove of garlic	2 teaspoons coriander powder
1 teaspoon turmeric	
1 teaspoon chilli powder (or less to taste)	1 tablespoon lemon juice
	2 tablespoons tomato purée

4 tablespoons oil or ghee	fresh coriander leaves or
salt and black pepper	parsley

Soak the beans overnight or pour boiling water over them and leave for an hour. Peel and chop the onions and garlic and fry in the oil until starting to brown.

Stir in the spices and continue to cook for a couple of minutes. Add the drained beans and stir well for a minute. Stir in the purée, seasoning and enough liquid to more than cover the beans. Simmer until tender or cook under pressure for 15 minutes.

Add the juice and leaves and serve with boiled rice and Turnips with Garlic (see p. 82).

BROWN LENTIL STEW

8 oz (230g) brown lentils	1 tablespoon lemon juice
3 onions	1 tablespoon soy sauce
1 carrot	salt and black pepper
2 large potatoes	2 fl. oz (100ml) oil
1 aubergine	stock
1 teaspoon yeast extract	

Pour a pint (550ml) of boiling water over the washed lentils and leave them to soak for an hour. Fry the chopped onions in the oil until starting to brown. Add the other vegetables chopped in fairly small pieces and stir well.

Add the lentils and their soaking water and enough stock to just cover everything. If using water add a stock cube. Bring to the boil and simmer until tender, or cook under pressure for 5 minutes.

Stir in the yeast extract, lemon juice and soy sauce, check the seasoning and serve with boiled rice.

CHANNA DAHL

12 oz (340g) channa dahl	$\frac{1}{2}$ teaspoon turmeric
(yellow split peas)	$\frac{1}{2}$ teaspoon cinnamon
1 onion	$\frac{1}{4}$ teaspoon clove powder
1 teaspoon mustard seeds	2 tablespoons lemon juice
$\frac{1}{2}$ teaspoon chilli powder	salt to taste
1 teaspoon ground black	2 tablespoons oil or ghee
pepper	

Pour boiling water on the washed dahl and leave to soak for an hour, then boil gently until soft. Heat the oil and fry the mustard seeds until they pop. Add the chopped onion and fry until starting to brown. Stir in the spices and continue to fry for a couple of minutes.

Remove from heat and stir in the cooked dahl. Add the lemon juice and salt and return to the heat for a few minutes before serving.

This dish should be served with rice and a vegetable side dish such as potato bahji. Alternatively, some boiled vegetable can be added to the dahl to make one substantial dish.

CHICK-PEA CASSEROLE

8 oz (230g) chick peas
2 onions
2 cloves of garlic
2 aubergines
3 courgettes
4 tomatoes

plenty of oil for frying
2 tablespoons tomato
  purée
$\frac{1}{2}$ teaspoon chilli powder
2 bay leaves
salt and black pepper

Soak the chick peas overnight or pour boiling water over them and leave for an hour. Cook until tender, about $\frac{3}{4}$ hour and drain. Dice the aubergines, sprinkle with salt and leave for some time, rinse and dry.

Heat some oil and fry the sliced courgettes until brown. Remove from pan and fry the aubergines until brown. Remove them also and fry the sliced onions and garlic until soft. Add the peeled, sliced tomatoes and chilli, and cook gently until soft. Add the bay leaves and the purée mixed in $\frac{1}{4}$ pint (150ml) water.

Combine all the ingredients, season well and place in a greased ovenproof dish. Cook in centre oven at 350°F — Mark 4 for 1 hour.

Try serving with Colcannon (p. 68).

CHILLI BEANS

12 oz (340g) red beans
3 onions
3 cloves of garlic

4 tomatoes
2 tablespoons tomato
  purée

1 red pepper
1 tablespoon paprika
½ teaspoon chilli powder
1 tablespoon soy sauce

2 bay leaves
3 tablespoons oil
salt and pepper

Soak the beans overnight, or pour on boiling water and leave them for an hour. Peel and chop the onion and garlic and fry in the oil until starting to brown.

Stir in the chilli powder and paprika, then the chopped tomatoes and pepper. Stir in the beans and their soaking liquid, adding more water or stock if necessary to cover them by at least an inch. Add the bay leaves and bring to the boil. Cook under pressure for about 20 minutes or simmer until beans are tender.

Stir in the tomato purée and season to taste, adding the soy sauce and more chilli if liked.

Try serving this dish with French Potatoes (p. 69) and Creamed Spinach (p. 69).

DAHL AMBROSIA

8 oz (230g) red lentils
2 onions
4 tomatoes
1 heaped teaspoon brown
  mustard seeds

1 tablespoon paprika
5 tablespoons oil
salt and black pepper
fresh coriander or parsley

Wash the lentils and cook in the minimum of water, watching carefully, until soft. Cool slightly and liquidize or sieve. Peel and chop the onions and fry in the oil until starting to brown. Add the mustard seeds and fry until they pop. Add the paprika and cook for another minute. Stir in the chopped tomatoes and cook at high heat until they become mushy.

Reduce heat and add the lentils. Simmer for about 10 minutes, season and serve garnished with chopped coriander or parsley.

Serve with Chappatis and Stir-Fry Tomatoes (p. 80).

HERBED LENTILS

12 oz (340g) brown lentils
2 onions

1 clove of garlic
2 sprigs fresh mint

1 sprig fresh sage
1 tablespoon lemon juice

salt and black pepper
3 tablespoons olive oil

Peel and chop the onions and garlic and fry gently in the oil for 5 minutes. Add the washed lentils, herbs and seasoning. Pour in about 2 pints (1 litre) water or stock and simmer very gently until tender.

Add the juice, check seasoning and serve with Fruit and Nut Rice (p. 60).

LENTIL PIE

12 oz (340g) red lentils
2 large potatoes
2 onions
1 lb (450g) tomatoes
2 oz (60g) margarine

a little soya milk
2 teaspoons curry powder
1 teaspoon yeast extract
salt and black pepper

Clean and soak the lentils and cook in just enough water until tender. Mash them, adding the curry powder, yeast extract and seasoning. At the same time boil and mash the potatoes with a little of the margarine and milk. Season with salt and lots of pepper.

Chop the onions and tomatoes and cook slowly in the rest of the margarine until thick and soft. Season.

In a greased ovenproof dish place the lentils, then the tomatoes and finally the mashed potatoes. Dot with margarine and bake at 375°F — Mark 5 for 30 minutes.

Try this dish with Stir-Fry Spinach (p. 79) or a green salad.

SOYA BEAN CURRY

12 oz (340g) split soya
  beans
2 onions
1 clove of garlic
3 tomatoes
2 tablespoons tomato purée
2 tablespoons lemon juice

$\frac{1}{2}$ teaspoon turmeric
2 teaspoons ground
  coriander
2 teaspoons curry powder
1 teaspoon garam masala
salt and black pepper
4 tablespoons oil or ghee

Split soya beans can be used without soaking, but will cook more quickly if soaked first.

Peel and chop onions and garlic and fry in the oil until starting to brown. Add the turmeric, coriander and curry powder and fry for a couple of minutes. Add the chopped tomatoes and cook for a few minutes more. Stir in the split beans, purée, juice and seasoning.

Add enough liquid, stock or water, to cover the beans, using more if they have not been soaked first. Simmer until the beans are tender. Stir in the garam masala before serving.

Try this dish with Fruit and Nut Rice (p. 60).

TOMATO BAKED BEANS

12 oz (340g) haricot beans
2 onions
2 cloves of garlic
4 tablespoons tomato
  purée
1 tablespoon soy sauce
1 tablespoon wine vinegar

2 tablespoons chopped
  parsley
2 bay leaves
$\frac{1}{2}$ teaspoon thyme
3 cloves
3 tablespoons olive oil
salt and black pepper

Soak the beans overnight or pour boiling water on them and leave for an hour. Simmer them until tender with the garlic, bay, thyme and 1 onion with the cloves or cook under pressure for 15 minutes or so. Drain the beans when cooked, keeping $\frac{1}{2}$ pint of the liquid. (Put the rest in the stock pot.)

Heat the oil and fry the other onion, chopped, until transparent. Add the tomato purée, bean liquid, parsley, soy sauce and seasoning.

Stir in the drained beans and turn into a greased ovenproof dish. The beans should be covered in sauce, so add a little more liquid if necessary. Cover and cook at 325°F — Mark 3 for 1 hour.

Try serving with Potato and Onion Fritters (p. 76) and Beans and Almonds (p. 66).

Nuts

BRAZIL BAKE

8 oz (230g) shelled Brazil nuts
2 onions
3 oz (90g) wholemeal
   breadcrumbs
2 oz (60g) margarine
1 tablespoon Tahini

1 tablespoon chopped
   parsley
1 green pepper
½ teaspoon marjoram
salt and black pepper

Grease an ovenproof dish. Mix half the crumbs with the Tahini and spread in the bottom of the dish. Melt half the margarine and fry the finely chopped onions and pepper gently for 10 minutes. Add the coarsely chopped nuts, herbs and seasoning and place on top of the crumb mixture. Top with the remaining crumbs, dot with the remaining margarine and bake at 375°F — Mark 5 for 30 minutes.

Serve with Hungarian Potatoes (p. 72) and a green salad.

LAZY NUT ROAST

1 onion
4 oz (120g) mushrooms
4 oz (120g) chopped or
   ground nuts
4 oz (120g) wholemeal
   breadcrumbs
1 tablespoon lemon juice

1 tablespoon chopped
   parsley
1 tablespoon oil
2 tablespoons tomato
   purée in half a mug of
   water
salt and black pepper

Chop the onion and mushrooms and mix well in bowl with all the other ingredients, adding more water if too dry. Turn into a greased ovenproof dish and bake at 300°F — Mark 2 for 1 hour.

Try serving with Potatoes and Mushrooms (p. 76) and a green salad.

MUSHROOM AND NUT ROAST

4 oz (120g) mushrooms
1 onion
3 sticks celery
3 oz (90g) chopped or
  ground nuts
2 oz (60g) wholemeal
  breadcrumbs
1 teaspoon yeast extract

½ teaspoon sage
1 tablespoon chopped
  parsley
2 oz (60g) margarine
3 teaspoons gram flour
  (see p. 132)
salt and black pepper

Chop the onion and celery finely and fry gently in the margarine for a few minutes. Add the sliced mushrooms and continue to cook slowly for 10 minutes. Add the nuts, crumbs, herbs, yeast extract and seasoning.

Sift the gram flour into a cup and mix to a thin paste with cold water. Add this to the roast mixture and place it in a greased ovenproof dish or tin. Bake at 375°F — Mark 5 for 30 minutes.

Serve with Hungarian Potatoes (p. 72) and a green vegetable.

NUT AND LENTIL ROAST

2 onions
4 oz (120g) red lentils
4 oz (120g) ground nuts
3 oz (90g) breadcrumbs
1 tablespoon wheatgerm
1 teaspoon mixed herbs

2 teaspoons yeast extract
1 tablespoon soy sauce
1 tablespoon lemon juice
2 oz (60g) margarine
salt and black pepper

Wash the lentils and cook in just enough water until tender. Chop the onion finely and cook gently in the margarine until starting to brown. Stir in all the remaining ingredients and turn into a greased ovenproof dish. Bake at 400°F — Mark 6 for 35 minutes. Try serving with Red Potatoes (p. 78), which can be cooked on the lower shelf of the oven, and Celery in Sauce (p. 68).

NUT CURRY

4 oz (120g) peanuts
4 oz (120g) cashew nuts
3 onions
3 tomatoes
2 oz (60g) dessicated
  coconut
1 teaspoon brown sugar
1 tablespoon lemon juice

4 tablespoons oil or ghee
$\frac{1}{2}$ teaspoon chilli powder
1 tablespoon Madras
  curry powder
salt and black pepper
fresh coriander or parsley
  leaves

Chop the onions and fry in the oil until starting to brown. Meanwhile mix the coconut with half a mug of water and leave to soak for a few minutes. Add the spices to it, mix well and stir this mixture into the onions.

Fry for a few minutes more, then add the chopped tomatoes, nuts, sugar and seasoning. Fry a little, then add enough stock or water to cover the nuts. Bring to the boil and simmer until nuts are tender and the sauce is thick.

Add the lemon juice, check the seasoning and serve garnished with the chopped leaves. Serve with Chappatis and Hot Tomato Salad (p. 87).

NUT LAYER SAVOURY

8 oz (230g) breadcrumbs
4 oz (120g) finely chopped
  nuts
4 oz (120g) mushrooms
8 oz (230g) tomatoes
4 oz (120g) margarine

1 teaspoon marjoram
1 tablespoon chopped
  parsley
1 tablespoon lemon juice
salt and black pepper

Fry the crumbs and nuts in 3 oz of the margarine. In the remaining margarine fry the chopped mushrooms and tomatoes until juicy. Add the lemon juice and seasoning. Put alternate layers of the two mixtures in a greased ovenproof dish, ending with the nut mix.

Bake for 30 minutes at 375°F — Mark 5, and serve with tomato sauce and greens.

A quick tomato sauce can be made with 2 tablespoons tomato purée to $\frac{3}{4}$ pint (400ml) of vegetable stock. Mix the two well, add a pinch of oregano and thyme, season with salt, black pepper and Worcestershire sauce. Simmer for two minutes.

NUT-STUFFED MUSHROOMS

1 lb (450g) large
   mushrooms
4 oz (120g) breadcrumbs
2 oz (60g) nuts: almond,
   Brazil or cashew

1 tablespoon chopped
   fresh parsley
1 tablespoon lemon juice
3 oz (90g) margarine
salt and black pepper

Clean the mushrooms and remove the stalks. Chop the stalks and mix with the crumbs, chopped nuts, parsley, juice, seasoning and 1 oz of the margarine, melted.

Stuff the mushroom caps with this mixture, place in a greased, shallow ovenproof dish, dot with the remaining margarine and cook at 350°F — Mark 4 for 20 minutes.

Try serving with Sweet and Sour Courgettes (p. 81) and Peas Pulao (p. 61).

PUREE OF CHESTNUTS EN CROUTE

Filling:
2 onions
1 clove of garlic
4 oz (120g) mushrooms
2 tomatoes
1 stick of celery
1 can chestnut purée
   (about 1 lb)
1 tablespoon lemon juice
½ teaspoon basil
2 oz (60g) margarine
salt and black pepper

Pastry:
12 oz (340g) flour, half
   81%, half wholemeal
6 oz (180g) margarine
1 teaspoon salt
½ teaspoon sugar
1 teaspoon lemon juice
ice-cold water

Rub margarine into flour, salt and sugar. Bind with juice and water. Roll out two-thirds of the pastry and line a 2lb loaf tin. Roll out the rest for the top.

Fry all the vegetables, finely chopped, except the tomatoes, in the margarine. When tender, but not brown, add a third of them to the chestnut purée. Mix well, adding the juice, basil and seasoning. Fill the tin with this mixture.

Meanwhile add the skinned and chopped tomatoes to the rest of the vegetables and fry quickly for 2 minutes. Season and spread on top of the chestnut mixture.

Dampen the edges of the pastry and cover with the remaining third. Make a cut in the centre. Bake at 350°F — Mark 4 for 45-50 minutes.

Serve with a wine sauce. (The recipe for a tomato sauce on p. 37 may be used — simply substitute $\frac{1}{4}$ (130ml) pint of red wine for $\frac{1}{4}$ (130ml) pint stock.)

 *Textured Vegetable Protein*

SOYA MEATBALLS

4 oz (120g) soya mince
2 onions
1 clove of garlic (optional)
1 oz (30g) margarine
1 teaspoon yeast extract
1 tablespoon soy sauce or
Holbrook's Worcestershire sauce

½ teaspoon mixed herbs
2 tablespoons gram flour
  (see p. 132)
2 tablespoons 81% flour
  (see p. 132)
plenty of oil for frying

Chop the onions and fry until tender in the margarine. Add the minced garlic, if liked. Add the mince, stir well and add just enough water or stock to be absorbed. Cook gently for 10 minutes, adding the herbs, yeast extract, sauce and seasoning. Allow to cool.

Sift the gram flour and add water to make a thick paste. Stir into the cooled mince, and form the mixture into balls. Roll in the flour and fry in the hot oil until golden brown.

Serve with a tomato or wine sauce and pasta or a rice dish and salad.

STIFATHO

1 packet Protoveg
  beef-flavoured chunks
8 oz (230g) button onions
3 tablespoons tomato
  purée
2 tablespoons cider
  vinegar
1 piece cinnamon stick

6 cloves
20 peppercorns
2 bay leaves
1 oz (30g) margarine
salt
stock
3 tablespoons oil

Soak the Protoveg for a few minutes in warm stock. Heat the oil and fry the drained Protoveg for 2 minutes. Add the spices, seasoning, purée and stock to cover. Simmer very slowly, uncovered, until the chunks are tender and the sauce well thickened.

Halfway through cooking time, brown the peeled onions in the margarine and add them to the Protoveg.

Serve with Fruit and Nut Rice (p. 60) and Peas with Mushrooms (p. 75).

SURPRISE PIE

4 oz (120g) soya meat
  chunks, beef flavoured
4 oz (120g) mushrooms
6 oz (180g) pastry
2 onions
1 oz (30g) margarine

1 level tablespoon plain
  flour
1 tablespoon paprika
1 stock cube
1 tablespoon soy sauce
salt and black pepper

Cook the soya meat as directed using the stock cube in the liquid. Make up the pastry and leave in fridge until required.

Fry the chopped onions in the margarine for a few minutes, add the sliced mushrooms and continue to cook gently for 5 minutes. Stir in the flour and paprika, cook for a minute then add the liquid from the cooked soya meat. Add the soy sauce and season well, then stir in the drained meat. Add more stock or water if the mixture seems too thick.

Turn into a greased pie dish, cool and cover with the pastry. Make a cut in the top, brush with soya milk if desired, and bake at 450°F — Mark 8 for about 20 minutes or until pastry looks cooked.

Serve with Petits Pois and new potatoes.

SWEET AND SOUR 'HAM'

1 packet Protoveg
  ham-flavoured chunks
2 onions
2 cloves of garlic
1 green pepper
1 small leek
2 oz (60g) margarine
1 oz (30g) flour

1 oz (30g) brown sugar
2 tablespoons lemon juice
1 small tin pineapple
  chunks
1 tablespoon tomato purée
2 teaspoons soy sauce
salt and black pepper

Cook the Protoveg as directed on packet. Meanwhile fry the onions and garlic, chopped finely, in the margarine, for a couple of minutes. Add the chopped pepper and leek and continue to fry for a few minutes without browning.

Stir in the flour then slowly add the liquid from the cooked Protoveg, the lemon juice and juice from the tin of pineapple. Stir in the sugar and flavourings, bring to the boil and simmer until the pepper is just tender.

Now add the Protoveg and pineapple chunks, reheat for a few minutes, check seasoning and serve with Fruit and Nut Rice (p. 60) and Petits Pois.

VEGAN SHEPHERD'S PIE

4 large potatoes	1 teaspoon yeast extract
1 oz (30g) margarine	1 tablespoon soy sauce
3 tablespoons soya milk	2 tablespoons tomato
2 mugfuls of soya mince	purée
2 onions	1 tablespoon paprika
1 carrot	½ teaspoon marjoram
½ green pepper	1 tablespoon wheatgerm
3 tablespoons oil	or oatflakes (optional)
1 vegetable stock cube	salt and black pepper

Peel and boil the potatoes and mash with a little margarine, seasoning and soya milk. Meanwhile gently fry the finely chopped vegetables in the oil for a few minutes. Stir in the paprika, then add the mince. Stir well then add as much stock or water as the mince will absorb, plus a little more. Add the cube and all the flavouring ingredients, and boil for 5 minutes.

Turn into a greased ovenproof dish, top with the mashed potato and sprinkle the wheatgerm or oatflakes (if liked) over the top. Dot with margarine and cook at 450°F — Mark 8 for about 15 minutes or till browned.

Serve with a crisp vegetable or salad.

VEGAN STEW

4 oz (120g) soya meat chunks,	2 onions
beef flavoured	2 potatoes

1 carrot
2 oz (60g) frozen peas
1 oz (30g) margarine
1 stock cube
1 teaspoon yeast extract

2 teaspoons paprika
1 oz (30g) plain flour
1 tablespoon lemon juice
1 tablespoon tomato purée
salt and black pepper

Warm 1 pint (550ml) of water with the stock cube, add the chunks and leave to soak as directed. Bring chunks to the boil and add the carrot and potato, chopped fairly small. Simmer with lid on for 5 minutes. Add the peas and continue to simmer until all is tender.

Meanwhile fry the chopped onions in the margarine until starting to brown. Stir in the paprika, then the flour. Drain in the stock from the cooked chunks, stirring well. Bring to the boil and add the yeast extract, juice, puree and seasoning.

Now gently stir in the drained chunks mixture and heat well for a few minutes.

Serve with boiled rice and Carrots and Cucumber (p. 67).

Vegetables

BAKED VEGETABLE ROLL

8 oz (230g) 81% plain
  flour
4 oz (120g) margarine
1 teaspoon lemon juice
1 teaspoon salt
a little water

Filling:
a variety of vegetables,
  e.g. onion, carrot, leek,
  celery, potato, tomato,
  mushroom (1 small
  onion, 1 carrot, $\frac{1}{2}$ head
  celery, 1 potato would
  be a good amount)

2 tablespoons minced
  nuts, or cooked lentils
  or beans
1 tablespoon chopped
  parsley
1 oz (30g) margarine
$\frac{1}{2}$ oz (15g) flour
1 teaspoon yeast extract
salt and black pepper

Rub margarine into flour and salt. Add juice and enough water to bind. Roll out very thinly into a square shape.

Mince the vegetables or break them down into tiny pieces in your liquidizer, straining off any liquid when you have finished. Melt the margarine and fry the vegetables gently for 10 minutes. Add the flour, nuts or beans, mashed, and seasoning.

When cool, spread the mixture on the pastry. Damp edges with water and roll the pastry into a roll, making sure the join is sealed and placed underneath. Seal the ends too. Brush the top with soya milk and mark a few slits in it.

Place on greased baking sheet and bake at 400°F — Mark 6 for about 40 minutes.

CAULIFLOWER SURPRISE CURRY

1 cauliflower
3 onions
4 tomatoes
3 firm pears
2 oz (60g) almonds or
  cashews
1 tablespoon curry
  powder

2 oz (60g) sultanas
1 tablespoon garam
  masala
1 tablespoon lemon juice
1 tablespoon tomato purée
3 tablespoons oil
salt and black pepper

Break cauliflower into florets and wash well. Chop the onions and fry in the oil until starting to brown. Add the curry powder then the chopped tomatoes and fry well for about 3 minutes. Add the sultanas, nuts and pears cut in chunks. Add the cauliflower and stir well.

Pour in enough water to come half way up the cauliflower and simmer until cauliflower is just tender, or cook under pressure for 4 minutes. When cooked, add the purée, lemon juice, garam masala and seasoning.

Serve with boiled rice and Chicory, Orange and Watercress Salad (p. 85).

FRUIT CURRY

3 large cooking apples
8 oz (230g) fresh apricots
2 bananas
2 oz (60g) raisins or
  sultanas
2 onions
1 teaspoon fresh ginger,
  chopped
juice and grated rind of 1
  lemon

1 tablespoon curry
  powder
2 oz (60g) coconut cream
3 tablespoons soured soya
  milk
$\frac{1}{2}$ teaspoon clove powder,
  or 5 cloves
1 tablespoon soya flour
salt to taste
4 tablespoons oil

Heat oil and fry chopped onion until starting to brown. Stir in curry powder, ginger, cloves and raisins, and fry for 2 minutes. Add coconut cream and flour. Now stir in the apples, peeled and cut in chunks, the halved apricots and sliced bananas.

Add enough water to just cover, and simmer until apples are

tender. Take care not to overcook. Now stir in the lemon, salt and milk.

Serve with boiled rice or Fruit and Nut Rice (p. 60).

(Soya milk is easily soured — just leave it in a warm place overnight.)

GREEN BANANA CURRY

4 large green bananas
3 onions
4 tomatoes
2 oz (60g) cashew nuts
1-2 tablespoons curry
   powder

1 tablespoon lemon juice
1 teaspoon fresh ginger,
   chopped
salt
3 tablespoons oil

Heat oil and fry chopped onion until starting to brown. Add ginger and curry powder, cook for another minute and add chopped tomatoes. Cook gently until thickened.

Peel only the very outer skin off the bananas, slice them and add. Stir well and add about ½ (275ml) pint of water. Simmer until bananas are tender.

Add juice, seasoning, and nuts just before serving.

MEDITERRANEAN MUSHROOMS

1 lb (450g) mushrooms
6 large tomatoes
3 cloves of garlic
1 teaspoon oregano or
   marjoram

2 bay leaves
2 teaspoons brown sugar
3 tablespoons olive oil
salt and black pepper

Slice the tomatoes and cook very gently in the oil with the sugar, seasoning and bay leaves. Keep the pan covered and stir occasionally.

After an hour remove the bay leaves, and liquidize or sieve the sauce. Return it to the pan and add the sliced mushrooms, garlic, crushed, and the oregano.

Simmer for 30 minutes, check seasoning and serve with pasta or boiled rice.

MEDITERRANEAN VEGETABLES

4 onions
3 cloves of garlic
3 green peppers
5 medium tomatoes
1 teaspoon oregano or
  marjoram

4 oz (120g) mushrooms
½ teaspoon sweet basil
dash of Tabasco sauce
3 tablespoons olive oil
salt and black pepper

Peel and chop onions and garlic and fry gently in oil until starting to brown. Add sliced peppers and peeled and sliced tomatoes, herbs and seasoning. Simmer until peppers are tender.

Slice the mushrooms and fry in hot oil for a minute or two. Add them to the pepper mixture, check seasoning and serve with boiled rice or pasta.

MUSHROOM CURRY

1 lb (450g) mushrooms
4 onions
5 tomatoes
2 cloves of garlic
½ teaspoon fresh ginger,
  minced
3 teaspoons Madras curry
  powder

½ teaspoon chilli powder
1 tablespoon lemon juice
salt
a few curry leaves, if
  available
chopped coriander leaves
  or parsley
4 tablespoons oil

Heat oil and fry chopped onions until starting to brown. Add chilli, curry powder and leaves and ginger. Cook for a minute, then add skinned, chopped tomatoes and crushed garlic.

Cook gently until thick, add mushrooms, halved if large, and continue to cook for 10 minutes, adding a little stock or water if getting dry.

Add lemon juice and salt to taste, and serve garnished with coriander leaves and accompanied by boiled rice.

MUSHROOM PIE

12 oz (340g) wholemeal
  flour
6 oz (180g) margarine

1 teaspoon salt
1 teaspoon lemon juice
water

Filling:
1 lb (450g) mushrooms
1 onion
4 sticks celery
2 oz (60g) cashew nuts
2 oz (60g) margarine
pinch thyme
salt and black pepper

Sauce:
1½ oz (50g) margarine
2 oz (60g) flour
½ pint (300ml) soya milk
salt, pepper and nutmeg

Make pastry as for Vegetable Pie (p. 53). Fry the chopped vegetables and nuts in the margarine for a few minutes and season.

Make the sauce by melting the margarine, stirring in the flour and adding the milk and seasoning. Add the mushroom mixture to the sauce.

Line the pie plate with pastry, pour in filling and cover with rest of pastry. Make slits in top. Bake at 350°F — Mark 4 for ½ hour or until browned.

Cool slightly before serving with green salad.

NETTLE PUDDING

1 lb (450g) young nettles
1 lb (450g) onions
4 oz (120g) oatmeal
3 tablespoons Smokey
 Snaps (see p. 133,
 optional)

1 oz (30g) margarine
stock
salt and black pepper

Wash the nettles well and chop them and the onions. Mix with the oatmeal, Smokey Snaps and seasoning. Add enough stock to moisten. Place in greased ovenproof dish, dot with margarine and bake at 325°F — Mark 3 for about 1 hour.

Try serving with Potatoes and Mushrooms (p. 76) and Stir-Fry Tomatoes (p. 80).

NUTTY STEW

8 oz (230g) onions
1 pepper
8 oz (230g) carrots
8 oz (230g) tomatoes
1 aubergine

4 oz (120g) frozen peas
4 tablespoons oil
2 tablespoons peanut
 butter or Tahini
2 teaspoons yeast extract

1 level tablespoon paprika
salt and pepper

1½ pints (850ml) stock or
water

Fry sliced onion and pepper in oil for a few minutes then stir in other vegetables, sliced, and the nut butter, paprika, yeast extract and liquid. Simmer until soft, stirring occasionally. Season and serve with rice or mashed potatoes.

PISTO

3 onions
1 clove of garlic
4 tomatoes
3 courgettes
2 peppers

8 oz (230g) new potatoes
1 tablespoon chopped
 parsley
4 tablespoons olive oil
salt and black pepper

Fry the finely chopped onions, garlic and parsley in the oil. Do not brown. Add the sliced peppers and continue to cook gently for about 10 minutes. Add the skinned, chopped tomatoes and sliced courgettes and cook slowly for about 30 minutes.

Scrape the potatoes, dice them, fry them quickly in a little hot oil and add them to the Pisto 10 minutes before the end of the cooking time. Season well and serve with Garlic Potatoes (p. 70) or Smokey Cauliflower (p. 78) and Wholemeal Bread (p. 117).

PIZZA

Base:
1 lb (450g) 81%
 self-raising flour
5 tablespoons oil
1½ teaspoons salt
oil for frying

Topping:
1 onion
1 clove of garlic
1 green pepper

4 tomatoes
4 oz (120g) mushrooms
2 tablespoons tomato
 purée
1 teaspoon marjoram
4 oz (120g) Vegan cheese
salt and black pepper
3 tablespoons oil

Stir the oil into the flour and salt. Add enough water to bind and knead for a minute or two. Roll out on floured board into 4 rounds. Heat a little oil in a heavy frying pan and fry each round on both sides until browned.

Cover with topping and place under a hot grill for about 2 minutes or until cheese starts to brown.

To make topping, fry the chopped onion, garlic and pepper in the oil for a few minutes, add the sliced tomatoes and mushrooms and cook a little longer, adding the marjoram and seasoning. Spread each pizza with tomato purée, add the topping and grate the cheese on top.

POTATO CURRY

4 large potatoes
4 tomatoes
2 oz (60g) margarine or
  ghee
1 teaspoon turmeric

1 teaspoon ground cumin
  seed
1 teaspoon chilli powder
  (vary to taste)
salt

Peel and dice the potatoes and chop the tomatoes. Melt the margarine and gently fry the potatoes, turmeric, cumin and salt for a few minutes. Add the tomatoes and chilli powder and fry for a couple of minutes more.

Stir in enough hot water to cover the potatoes, bring to the boil and simmer gently till the potatoes are tender.

Serve with rice.

POTATO STEW

4 large potatoes
2 onions
2 cloves of garlic
2 oz (60g) margarine
½ teaspoon marjoram or
  sage

2 tablespoons olive oil
1 tablespoon wine vinegar
½ pint (300ml) stock
salt and black pepper
parsley

Peel and chop the onions and garlic and fry gently in the margarine in a large pan. When onion is transparent, add the peeled and diced potatoes and stir well to coat them in fat. Pour in enough stock to almost cover the potatoes, add the herbs and seasoning.

Simmer for about 40 minutes, or until potatoes are tender. Add the oil and vinegar.

Serve garnished with chopped parsley and eat with Chappatis (p. 59) or bread and salad.

RATATOUILLE

1 large onion	$\frac{1}{2}$ pint (300ml) stock
2 cloves of garlic	$\frac{1}{2}$ teaspoon oregano or
2 green peppers	marjoram
1 aubergine	2 bay leaves
3 medium courgettes	1 teaspoon brown sugar
4 tomatoes	salt and black pepper
4 tablespoons olive oil	parsley
2 tablespoons tomato purée	

Dice the aubergine, cover with salt, leave for $\frac{1}{2}$ hour and rinse.

Heat oil in a large, thick pan and gently fry the peeled and sliced onion, minced garlic and sliced peppers. Add the diced aubergine and sliced courgettes, and fry a few minutes more. Add the herbs, seasoning and stock mixed with the tomato purée.

Cook slowly until the sauce has nearly disappeared and the vegetables are just tender. Add the sliced tomatoes a few minutes before removing from the stove.

Check seasoning and serve hot or cold garnished with chopped parsley and accompanied by hot French bread or freshly baked wholemeal bread. If serving cold, stir in 2 tablespoons French dressing before serving.

STUFFED CABBAGE LEAVES

8 large but young cabbage leaves	2 oz (60g) margarine
2 onions	2 oz (60g) chopped nuts
1 lb (450g) tomatoes	1 teaspoon mixed herbs
2 oz (60g) breadcrumbs or cooked rice	1 teaspoon lemon juice
	salt and black pepper

Boil the leaves for a few minutes until tender, drain and flatten. Put three-quarters of the tomatoes, sliced, in a large casserole. Fry the rest of the chopped onion in the margarine until thick. Stir in the rice or crumbs, the herbs and nuts. Season, then divide the mixture between the leaves.

Roll them up and tie with cotton. Place the rolls on top of the tomatoes, dot with margarine, cover and cook for about an hour in a moderate oven 325°F — Mark 3.

STUFFED PEPPERS

4 large green peppers
1 onion
1 clove of garlic
4 oz (120g) rice
2 oz (60g) margarine

1 tablespoon chopped
  parsley
1 tablespoon tomato purée
$\frac{3}{4}$ pint (400ml) stock

Remove tops from washed peppers and scoop out the seeds and discard them. Melt the margarine and fry the chopped onion and garlic for a few minutes. Add the rice and fry a little longer. Stir in the hot stock, bring to the boil and simmer with salt and pepper to taste until the rice is tender.

Cool, add parsley and stuff the peppers, replacing the tops. Place in greased baking dish, and surround with $\frac{1}{2}$ pint (300ml) water mixed with the tomato purée.

Bake covered for 30 minutes at 350°F — Mark 4, then remove cover, baste, and cook for 15 minutes more.

Serve with Hungarian Potatoes (p. 72) and salad.

STUFFED TOMATOES

8 medium-sized tomatoes
2 oz (60g) margarine or
  ghee
1 onion
1½ cups boiled rice

$\frac{1}{2}$ teaspoon turmeric
$\frac{1}{2}$ teaspoon garam masala
salt
few leaves fresh coriander
  or parsley

Cut the tops off the washed tomatoes, and scoop out the seed pulp. Fry the chopped onion in the margarine. When starting to brown, add the spices and tomato pulp and continue to cook for a few minutes. Stir in the cooked rice and chopped coriander and cool.

Stuff the tomatoes with the mixture, put on the lids, place in greased baking dish and bake at 350°F — Mark 4 for 10-15 minutes.

This dish goes well with a green vegetable, e.g. creamed spinach and a potato dish like Potatoes and Mushrooms (p. 76).

VEGETABLE HOT-POT

2 onions
2 carrots
2 small leeks
4 sticks celery
1 turnip *or* 4 Jerusalem
  artichokes
2 tomatoes
2 oz (60g) fresh or frozen
  peas or green beans

2 large potatoes
2 oz (60g) margarine
2 tablespoons tomato
  purée
1 teaspoon yeast extract
1 pint (550ml) stock
salt and black pepper
2 bay leaves
parsley

Clean, peel and chop the first five vegetables, then fry them for a minutes in half the margarine. Pour in the stock, add the tomato purée, yeast extract, bay leaves and seasoning and bring to the boil.

Place sliced tomatoes in a greased ovenproof dish, add the peas or beans, then the vegetable mixture. Cover the top with the peeled and sliced potatoes. Dot with rest of the margarine, cover and cook at 400°F — Mark 6 for 45 minutes, remove lid and cook another 15 minutes.

Sprinkle with chopped parsley and serve.

VEGETABLE PIE

Pastry:
12 oz (340g) wholemeal
  flour
6 oz (180g) margarine
1 teaspoon salt
1 teaspoon lemon juice
water

Filling:
4 oz (120g) tomatoes
2 large potatoes
4 oz (120g) onions
6 oz (180g) mushrooms
½ oz (15g) margarine
salt and black pepper
pinch of favourite herb

Rub margarine into flour, then bind with juice and water. Roll out thinly and line a greased pie plate with just over half the pastry. Put in layer of sliced tomatoes, then thinly sliced potatoes. Top with the onions and mushrooms which can be fried lightly first. Season and dot with margarine.

Cover with rest of pastry, using water to seal the edges, and cutting four slits in the top to let the steam escape. Bake at 350°F — Mark 4 for about 1 hour or until browned. Serve with salad.

 *Pasta*

NEAPOLITAN SPAGHETTI

1 lb (450g) spaghetti
6 cloves of garlic
½ pint (300ml) olive oil

3 tablespoons chopped
parsley or other fresh
herb

Boil the spaghetti in plenty of salted water; drain. Warm the oil and add the garlic cloves, well crushed. Stir them around for a minute or two then pour the oil over the spaghetti and sprinkle the parsley on top. Serve with a variety of colourful salads.

NUTTY SPAGHETTI

1 lb (450g) wholemeal
  spaghetti
2 onions
3 oz (90g) sultanas
2 tablespoons tomato
  purée
3 tablespoons peanut
  butter

1 teaspoon yeast extract
1 tablespoon curry
  powder
1 tablespoon lemon juice
3 tablespoons oil
salt and black pepper
salted peanuts and cress or
  parsley for garnish

Boil the spaghetti in plenty of salted water and drain. Chop the onions and fry in the oil until they start to brown. Add the curry powder, then the other ingredients and enough water to make a fairly thick sauce.

Heat well and serve garnished with the nuts and cress, on top of the spaghetti or in a separate dish. A salad such as Chicory, Orange and Watercress (p. 85) goes well with this dish.

PASTA WITH BEANS

8 oz (230g) haricot beans
6 oz (180g) wholemeal
  spaghetti rings
6 tablespoons olive oil
2 cloves of garlic
1 bay leaf
1 onion

2 carrots
1 stick of celery
5 tomatoes
1 teaspoon marjoram
$\frac{1}{2}$ teaspoon basil
salt and black pepper
parsley

Soak the beans overnight or pour 2 pints (1 litre) boiling water over them and leave for an hour. Add 3 tablespoons of the oil, 1 clove of garlic, the bay leaf and some salt and simmer the beans until tender, or cook under pressure.

Chop the onion, carrots and celery finely and fry gently in the rest of the oil with the other clove of garlic, minced, and the herbs and seasoning. Add the skinned, sliced tomatoes after 30 minutes and cook for another 15 minutes.

Cook the pasta in plenty of boiling, salted water and drain. Combine the pasta, drained beans and vegetable mixture, adding $\frac{1}{2}$ pint of the bean liquid.

Heat through, check seasoning and serve garnished with chopped parsley.

SPAGHETTI AUBERGINE

1 lb (450g) wholemeal
  spaghetti
1 large aubergine
2 cloves of garlic
2 green peppers
6 tomatoes

4 tablespoons tomato
  purée
1 teaspoon oregano
$\frac{1}{2}$ teaspoon basil
4 tablespoons olive oil
salt and black pepper

Heat the oil and add to it the crushed garlic, peeled and chopped tomatoes and finely chopped aubergine and peppers. Fry gently for a few minutes, then add the purée, herbs, seasoning and about $\frac{1}{2}$ pint water, stock or wine. Simmer with the lid on, stirring occasionally, for about 40 minutes, adding more liquid if necessary.

Whilst the sauce is cooking, boil the spaghetti in plenty of salted water and drain. Serve separately with a green vegetable or salad.

SPAGHETTI BOLOGNESE

1 lb (450g) wholemeal
  spaghetti
2 onions
2 cloves of garlic
3 tomatoes
4 oz (120g) soya mince
2 tablespoons tomato
  purée

1 teaspoon marjoram
2 bay leaves
2 teaspoons Holbrook's
  Worcestershire sauce
3 tablespoons olive oil
salt and black pepper
parsley

Boil the spaghetti in plenty of salted water, drain and keep hot.
Fry the finely chopped vegetables in the oil for a few minutes. Add
the mince, stir and add about ½ pint of water or stock, the herbs,
purée and seasoning. Simmer for 10 minutes, adding more liquid
if necessary.

Add the Worcestershire sauce, check seasoning and serve
garnished with chopped parsley. For special occasions, add a little
wine whilst cooking the sauce.

Try serving with Lettuce and Courgette Salad (p. 88).

(Holbrook's is the only vegan Worcestershire sauce, as it con-
tains no anchovies, which other brands do.)

SPAGHETTI SURPRISE

1 lb (450g) wholemeal
  spaghetti
3 onions
1 clove of garlic
3 large carrots
1 green pepper

4 tablespoons tomato purée
1 teaspoon brown sugar
1 teaspoon marjoram
½ teaspoon basil
4 tablespoons olive oil
salt and black pepper

Boil spaghetti in plenty of salted water, drain and keep hot. Chop
the onions and pepper finely, crush the garlic and grate the carrots
on a coarse grater. Heat the oil and fry all the vegetables gently for
10 minutes.

Stir in the purée, herbs, sugar and seasoning and enough water
to make a thick sauce. Simmer for about 20 minutes, adjusting
seasoning and adding more liquid if necessary.

Serve separately with Petits Pois or a green salad.

TAGLIATELLE

1 lb (450g) tagliatelle
4 tablespoons
    breadcrumbs
4 tablespoons margarine

2 tablespoons poppy seeds
1 tablespoon Smokey
    Snaps (see p. 133)

Cook the tagliatelle in plenty of salted, boiling water until tender. Drain it well. Fry the crumbs in the margarine until just browned. Stir in the poppy seeds and Smokey Snaps. Sprinkle this mixture over the tagliatelle and serve immediately.

This goes well with any tomato sauce.

It is important to check the ingredients on packets of tagliatelle, as some brands contain egg ('uovo' in Italian).

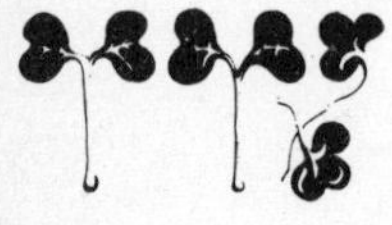 # Cereal Dishes 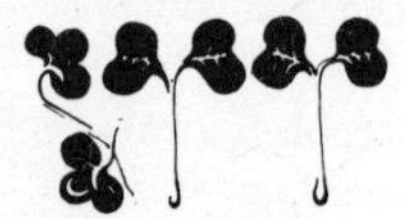

BUCKWHEAT SPECIAL

8 oz (230g) buckwheat
2 small onions
2 tomatoes
4 oz (120g) mushrooms
1 stick of celery

1 tablespoon lemon juice
1 tablespoon soy sauce
3 oz (90g) margarine
salt and black pepper
parsley

If the buckwheat is unroasted, stir it in a thick pan over medium heat for a few minutes. Then boil the buckwheat in twice its quantity of water or stock for about 15 minutes, or until tender.

Meanwhile, chop the vegetables and fry gently in the margarine for 10 minutes. Add the buckwheat when it is cooked and stir in the juice, soy sauce and seasoning.

Finally add some chopped parsley and sprinkle more on top. This is a pleasant and nutritious change from rice and goes well with foods which are sauce-based.

BULGUR

8 oz (230g) bulgur
2 onions
1 pint (550ml) stock or
  water
1 tablespoon soy sauce

1 tablespoon lemon juice
2 teaspoons yeast extract
salt and black pepper
3 tablespoons oil

Chop onions and fry in oil until starting to brown. Add the bulgur and stir well for a minute. Add 1 pint (550ml) stock or water and bring to the boil, stirring. Simmer for about 15 minutes or until tender, adding more water if necessary and stirring occasionally.

Add the juice, sauce, yeast extract and seasoning to taste before serving. Bulgur makes a pleasant change from rice or potatoes. For variety, try adding some curry powder, or a spoonful of your favourite herbs.

CHAPPATIS

12 oz (340g) chappati
  flour or 81% flour

1 teaspoon salt
ghee or margarine

Place flour and salt in a large bowl and add sufficient water to make a pliable dough. Cover with a damp cloth and leave for an hour or longer. Take lumps of dough, knead well and roll out into rounds on a floured board.

Heat a thick-bottomed pan or thawa and cook the chappati for a few moments on one side. Turn it and cook on second side until brown spots start to appear. Turn back to first side and press the edges with a clean cloth to make the chappati rise up.

Remove from pan and spread with ghee or margarine on one side if liked. Keep the cooked chappatis wrapped in a cloth, to keep them hot and soft. Serve as soon as all are cooked.

A thawa is a curved pan used for cooking chappatis. They are sold in many Indian grocery stores.

CHINESE FRIED RICE

12 oz (340g) cooked,
  brown rice
2 onions
1 clove of garlic
2 sticks of celery
1 carrot

2 oz (60g) mushrooms
2 oz (60g) bean sprouts
1-2 tablespoons soy sauce
1 teaspoon lemon juice
salt and black pepper
4 tablespoons oil

Heat oil in a large frying pan and fry the crushed garlic for a minute, add the sliced onion and continue to cook gently. Turn up the heat and add the carrot, cut in thin strips, and chopped celery and mushrooms. Cook quickly, stirring, for 2-3 minutes.

Now add the bean sprouts, juice, soy sauce and seasoning. Stir in the cooked rice and serve sprinkled with soy sauce. It is best to add the rice while it is hot, so if you have cooked it some time before, reheat it in a colander over boiling water.

FRUIT AND NUT RICE

12 oz (340g) brown rice, cooked
1 onion
8 oz (230g) chopped dried fruit
4 oz (120g) chopped almonds or walnuts
2 oz (60g) sesame seeds
½ teaspoon clove powder
½ teaspoon cinnamon
2 oz (60g) margarine
about 3 tablespoons oil
salt
1 tablespoon lemon juice

Heat oil and gently fry chopped onion until golden. Add fruit and nuts, spices and salt. Cook a few minutes more, then stir gently into the cooked rice, adding the juice of the lemon now.

Turn into a greased casserole, cover with the melted margarine, and heat through for 15 minutes in a moderate oven, 350°F — Mark 4.

Alternatively, you can add the rice to the fruit pan and heat through on top of your cooker. This is quicker, but be careful not to get your rice in a mush!

PAELLA

8 oz (230g) rice
4 tablespoons olive oil
3 onions
1 clove of garlic
3 tomatoes
4 oz (120g) peas
2 sticks of celery
1 red pepper
2 heaped tablespoons salted cashew nuts
rind and juice 1 lemon
1 tablespoon chopped parsley
1 teaspoon marjoram
1 teaspoon turmeric (or a pinch of saffron)
1 tablespoon soy sauce
1 pint (550ml) hot stock
salt and black pepper

Gently fry the rice in the oil in a large, thick pan until slightly yellow. Add the finely chopped onions and garlic and fry for a few minutes more. Stir in the turmeric, then add the skinned, chopped tomatoes and the hot stock or water. Bring to the boil and simmer, covered, for 5 minutes.

Add the peas, continue to cook. After 10 minutes add the chopped celery and sliced pepper. Continue to cook until rice is tender and liquid absorbed, adding more hot liquid if necessary. Gently stir in the herbs, nuts, lemon rind and juice, soy sauce, salt and pepper.

Serve at once, or keep covered in a low oven. You can garnish this dish with black olives, parsley or nuts and tomatoes.

PARATHAS (FRIED CHAPPATIS)

12 oz (340g) chappati
  flour or 81% flour
  (self-raising is good)

1 teaspoon salt
plenty of ghee, margarine
  or oil

Place flour and salt in bowl, add enough water to make a pliable dough and leave for an hour, covered with a damp cloth. Roll out into rounds on a floured board and spread with margarine on one side.

Fold in half, press the edges and spread with margarine again. Fold in half again and roll out into fan shapes.

Heat a thick-bottomed pan and fry lightly on both sides, then add a little margarine to the pan and fry on both sides until nicely browned. Serve hot.

PEAS PULAO

8 oz (230g) rice
8 oz (230g) peas, shelled
  or frozen
2 cloves of garlic
1 teaspoon caraway seeds
$\frac{1}{2}$ teaspoon turmeric
4 cloves

$\frac{1}{2}$ teaspoon cinnamon
1 tablespoon lemon juice
3 tablespoons oil
$\frac{3}{4}$ pint (400ml) hot stock or
  water
salt and black pepper

Fry the spices and minced garlic in the oil over a low heat for a couple of minutes. Add the rice and cook, stirring, for a few minutes. Add the peas and stir in the hot stock and seasoning. If using frozen peas, add them half-way through the cooking time or they will go mushy. Cover and cook slowly until rice and peas are tender and liquid absorbed. Add more hot water if necessary.

Stir in the lemon juice and check seasoning before serving. This dish goes well with most curries.

PURIS

12 oz (340g) 81%
  self-raising flour
1 teaspoon salt

3 oz (90g) margarine
plenty of ghee or oil for
  frying

Rub margarine into flour and salt, add enough water to make a pliable dough and knead for a few minutes. Roll out into one large round and spread with ghee, oil or margarine. Fold over and roll out very thinly.

Heat plenty of oil in a thick pan. Cut out circles of dough about 3" in diameter and drop them into the oil. Press down with a spoon and they should puff up. Turn over as soon as the first side is golden brown and cook second side. Drain and keep hot and serve as soon as possible.

Puris are a little troublesome to make and cook but will be greeted with such delight that the enterprise will surely seem worthwhile!

QUICK VEGETABLE RICE

8 oz (230g) cooked rice
  (left-overs)
4 oz (120g) mushrooms
1 tablespoon chopped
  parsley

4 large tomatoes
1 tablespoon soy sauce
$\frac{1}{2}$ teaspoon marjoram
salt and black pepper
4 tablespoons oil

Heat the oil and fry the chopped mushrooms and tomatoes quickly for a few minutes. Add the herbs, soy sauce and seasoning and stir in the rice. Lower the heat and allow to warm through gently. Check seasoning and serve.

QUICK YELLOW RICE

8-12 oz (230-340g) cooked
  rice

2 onions
2 tablespoons sultanas

2 tablespoons broken
  cashew nuts
1 tablespoon Smokey
  Snaps (see p. 133)
½ teaspoon cinnamon

4 cloves
½ teaspoon turmeric
4 tablespoons oil
1 tablespoon lemon juice
salt and black pepper

Fry the chopped onions in the oil until nearly brown. Stir in the sultanas and allow to plump up. Add the spices, nuts and Smokey Snaps. Stir the rice in gently, add the lemon juice, season and heat through before serving. This goes well with curry dishes.

RISOTTO

8 oz (230g) rice
1 onion
1 clove of garlic (optional)
4 tablespoons olive oil

salt and black pepper
¾ pint (400ml) hot water or
  stock
parsley

Gently fry chopped onion and minced garlic in the oil in a large, thick pan. Stir in the rice and continue to cook until golden. Add ½ pint hot water, bring to the boil and simmer, covered, until tender. Add more hot water if necessary.

Season well and garnish with chopped parsley. To add a luxury taste to this dish, replace some of the stock with white wine.

Side Dishes

These dishes are intended to accompany the main dish. For example, a stir-fry vegetable will go well with a heavy main dish such as a nut roast. A clever choice of side dish will add colour, flavour and texture to the meal, as well as goodness. Several recipes advise the use of olive oil. This oil does add a special flavour to foods, but it has two disadvantages — a high price and a high saturated fat content. Those who wish to cut down their fat intake for health or dietary reasons should use any other vegetable oil instead. Sunflower oil is a popular substitute.

AUBERGINE FRITTERS

3 small aubergines or 2
  large ones
1 clove of garlic (optional)
1 teaspoon garam masala

2 tablespoons gram flour
  (see p. 132)
salt and black pepper
plenty of oil for frying

Wash the aubergines and cut in fairly thin slices. Rub each slice with the cut clove of garlic. Sift the gram flour, add the spice and seasoning and enough water to make a thick batter.

Heat the oil, dip each aubergine slice in the batter and fry until golden brown on both sides. Serve hot.

BEANS AND ALMONDS

1 lb (450g) fresh or frozen
  green beans
3 oz (90g) margarine

2 oz (60g) almonds
2 tablespoons lemon juice
salt and black pepper

String and cut the beans and cook in boiling, salted water until tender. Drain. Melt the margarine and fry the blanched, sliced almonds until they are slightly browned. Add the juice and seasoning and pour over the cooked beans. Serve at once.

BEETROOT SPECIAL

4 freshly cooked beetroot,
  sliced
$\frac{1}{2}$ pint (300ml) red grape
  juice
1 tablespoon lemon juice
2 oz (60g) margarine
1 tablespoon flour

1 teaspoon brown sugar
$\frac{1}{4}$ teaspoon nutmeg
  (freshly grated if
  possible)
$\frac{1}{4}$ teaspoon clove powder
salt and black pepper

Melt the margarine, add flour then stir in grape juice. Bring to the boil, stirring, then add all the other ingredients and simmer for 10 minutes. Check seasoning and serve.

CABBAGE WITH COCONUT

1 cabbage
2 onions

1 clove of garlic
1 teaspoon minced ginger

½ teaspon chilli powder
½ coconut grated (or 3
  tablespoons dessicated
  coconut soaked in water
  for 10 minutes)

1 teaspoon salt
black pepper
4 tablespoons oil or ghee

Peel and chop the onions and garlic and fry with the ginger in the oil. After a few minutes add the chilli and then the finely shredded cabbage and salt. Fry, stirring, over medium heat.

When nearly done stir in the coconut and continue to cook until tender. Check seasoning and sprinkle with black pepper before serving.

CARROTS AND CUCUMBERS

1 cucumber
8 oz (230g) new carrots
1 tablespoon chopped
  parsley

½ oz (15g) margarine
1 teaspoon brown sugar
salt and black pepper

Peel the cucumber, cut it in half lengthways and then across in ½-inch slices. Plunge in boiling salted water for a minute, drain and place in a bowl of cold water.

Scrape the carrots, quarter them and cook with the sugar, margarine and a little salt in enough water to just cover. Keep covered until just tender, then remove lid and continue to cook until the water has evaporated.

Add the cucumber, parsley and black pepper and stir well. Serve at once.

CARROTS AND ONIONS IN SAUCE

3 large onions
4 large carrots
2 oz (60g) margarine

1½ oz (45g) flour
salt and black pepper

Peel and slice vegetables and cook in a pint (550ml) of water until tender. Drain, reserving liquid. Melt margarine in pan, stir in flour and add vegetable liquid slowly, stirring. Bring to the boil, season well and add carrots and onions. Heat through and serve hot.

CARROTS DEBORAH

4 carrots
1 oz (30g) margarine
½ teaspoon salt

1 level tablespoon brown
  sugar

Grate the carrots and place all ingredients in pan with about ¼ pint (150ml) of water. Simmer gently until carrots are tender and water absorbed. You may have to add a little more water to prevent drying out. Serve hot.

CELERY IN SAUCE

1 head of celery
1 oz (30g) margarine

1 oz (30g) flour
salt and black pepper

Wash the celery well and cut into 1-inch pieces, removing any strings. Bring ¾ pint (420ml) water, salted, to the boil, add the celery and simmer until tender. Drain, reserving the liquid.

In the rinsed pan melt the margarine, stir in the flour and slowly stir in the celery liquid. Bring to the boil and season with black pepper.

Add the celery, heat through and serve.

COLCANNON

1½ lb (670g) potatoes
8 oz (230g) cabbage
1 bunch spring onions

2 oz (60g) margarine
¼ pint (150ml) soya milk
salt and black pepper

Peel, boil and mash the potatoes and shred and boil the cabbage. Chop the onions and bring to the boil in the soya milk. Melt the margarine, add the drained cabbage, then the milk and onions. Finally, stir in the mashed potato and plenty of seasoning.

Serve hot, perhaps with a garnish of Smokey Snaps (see p. 133).

CONTINENTAL GREEN BEANS

1 lb (450g) runner beans
1 onion
1 lb (450g) tomatoes
1 teaspoon chopped mint

1 tablespoon chopped
  parsley
4 tablespoons olive oil
salt and black pepper

Wash, string and slice the beans and cook in just enough water to cover for 8 minutes or until just tender. Slice the onion, skin and chop the tomatoes and add together with the oil, mint and seasoning. Cover and simmer for 30 minutes, stirring occasionally.

Serve garnished with the parsley.

COURGETTES NICOISE

1 lb (450g) courgettes
8 oz (230g) tomatoes
1 clove of garlic
6 stoned black olives
½ teaspoon marjoram

1 tablespoon chopped
  parsley
3 tablespoons olive oil
salt and black pepper

Cut the courgettes in ¼-inch slices, sprinkle with salt and leave for 10 minutes. Wipe them dry and fry them gently in the oil with the crushed garlic until tender. Add the skinned and chopped tomatoes and continue to cook until almost a sauce.

Season well, add the herbs and serve.

CREAMED SPINACH

1-1½ lb (450-670g) spinach
1 oz (30g) margarine

1 tablespoon flour
salt and black pepper

Wash spinach thoroughly, remove thickest stalks and tear large leaves. Bring ¼ pint water to the boil with a little salt, add spinach and cook with lid on for about 5 minutes.

Drain spinach, reserving liquid. Melt margarine in pan, stir in flour and add spinach liquid slowly, stirring all the time. Boil for a minute, season and add the spinach. Heat through and serve hot.

FRENCH POTATOES

1½ lb (670g) potatoes
2 tablespoons chopped
  chives
2 tablespoons French
  mustard

1 tablespoon chopped
  parsley
1 oz (30g) margarine
½ pint (300ml) stock
salt and black pepper

Peel the potatoes and cut into fairly thick slices. Layer them in a greased ovenproof dish, sprinkling the herbs between the layers of potato. Blend the mustard, stock and seasoning and pour over the potatoes. Melt the margarine and pour it on top, cover, and bake at 350°F — Mark 4 for 1½-2 hours until cooked.

FRUITY CAULIFLOWER

1 large cauliflower
2 tablespoons orange juice
1 tablespoon lemon juice

1 oz (30g) margarine
1 oz (30g) flour
salt and black pepper

Wash cauliflower well, break into large florets and boil in ½ pint water or stock until just tender. Drain, reserving the liquid. Melt the margarine, stir in flour then stir in the cauliflower liquid and juices. Boil for 2 minutes, season to taste and pour over cauliflower and serve.

FRUITY PARSNIPS

2 lb (900g) parsnips
4 tablespoons orange juice
1 tablespoon lemon juice
3 tablespoons brown sugar

1 teaspoon salt
1 teaspoon chopped fresh
　mint
2 oz (60g) margarine

Peel the parsnips, boil until tender, drain and slice. Mix the other ingredients, keeping a little margarine aside, and melting the rest for easy mixing. In a shallow, greased, ovenproof dish place alternate layers of parsnips and liquid. Dot with the remaining margarine and bake at 375°F — Mark 5 for about 20 minutes.

GARLIC POTATOES

4 very large or 8 medium
　potatoes
3 oz (90g) margarine
3 cloves of garlic

1 tablespoon chopped
　parsley
salt and black pepper

Peel the potatoes and cut in fairly thick slices, down to, but not through the base. Stand each one on a square of kitchen foil. Melt the margarine, add the crushed garlic and seasoning and pour over the potatoes, seeing that some goes between each slice. Wrap loosely in the foil, sealing the edges. Place the foil parcels on a baking sheet and bake in centre oven for about 45 minutes at 425°F — Mark 7. Uncover the top of each parcel before serving and sprinkle with parsley.

GREEK MUSHROOMS

1 lb (450g) mushrooms
3 tablespoons tomato
  purée
1 onion

1 clove of garlic
2 tablespoons olive oil
½ teaspoon basil
salt and black pepper

Chop the onion and garlic and fry gently in the oil for a few minutes. Stir in the purée mixed with ½ pint water. Season and simmer slowly with the basil for 30 minutes. Clean and slice the mushrooms, add to pan and simmer for 10 minutes more. Check seasoning and serve.

GREEK PEPPERS

4 green peppers
1 onion
1 clove of garlic
4 tomatoes
2 tablespoons tomato purée

½ teaspoon marjoram
3 tablespoons olive oil
salt and black pepper

Gently fry the finely chopped onion and garlic in the oil for a few minutes. Add the skinned and chopped tomatoes, the purée and ¼ pint (130ml) water or stock. Simmer for 5 minutes, then add the peppers cut in thin strips and the marjoram and seasoning.

Cover and simmer for about 30 minutes or until tender, stirring occasionally and adding more liquid if necessary. Check seasoning and serve.

GUJERATI POTATOES

1 lb (450g) potatoes
2 green chillies
½ oz (15g) tamarind (or 1
  tablespoon vinegar)

1 tablespoon brown sugar
4 tablespoons oil or ghee
1 teaspoon black mustard
  seeds

$\frac{1}{2}$ teaspoon turmeric
$\frac{1}{2}$ teaspoon chilli powder
2 teaspoons coriander
　powder

2 tablespoons dessicated
　coconut
salt

Put the tamarind in 3 tablespoons hot water, leave for 10 minutes, squeeze it and strain the liquid for use, adding the sugar to it. Heat the oil and fry the mustard seeds until they pop. Add the peeled, diced potatoes and all the spices, fry for 2 minutes.

Reduce heat, cover and cook slowly until potatoes are cooked. Stir in the tamarind juice, chopped green chillies and coconut and cook for another 5 minutes.

HUNGARIAN POTATOES

4 large potatoes
2 onions
2 tomatoes
1 tablespoon paprika
3 tablespoons oil

2 bay leaves
1 tablespoon tomato purée
stock
salt and black pepper
parsley

Peel and slice the onions and fry in the oil for a few minutes. Add the paprika, then the skinned and sliced tomatoes. Peel the potatoes, slice fairly thickly and add. Stir well, then pour in enough stock to cover, add the bay leaves and purée, transfer to an ovenproof dish and cook at 375°F — Mark 5 for about one hour or until tender. Serve garnished with chopped parsley.

INDIAN CAULIFLOWER WITH PEAS

1 cauliflower
1 lb (450g) fresh peas (or
　$\frac{1}{2}$ lb (230g) frozen)
1 teaspoon minced ginger
2 green chillies
$\frac{1}{2}$ teaspoon caraway seeds
$\frac{1}{2}$ teaspoon turmeric

$\frac{1}{2}$ teaspoon coriander
　powder
1 tablespoon chopped
　coriander leaves or
　parsley
3 tablespoons oil or ghee
salt and black pepper

Heat the oil and fry the ginger and seeds for a couple of minutes. Add the cauliflower, broken up into florets, and the fresh peas, shelled. If using frozen peas, add them halfway through the cooking time. Fry a little longer, then stir in the chillies, turmeric, coriander powder and seasoning. Add ¼ pint water and simmer, stirring occasionally, until cooked. Serve garnished with the chopped leaves.

JERUSALEM ARTICHOKES IN SAUCE

1½ lb (670g) artichokes
1 onion
1 clove of garlic
2 oz (60g) margarine
¼ teaspoon nutmeg

1 bouquet garni
1 tablespoon lemon juice
2 tablespoons cornflour
1 pint (550ml) stock
salt and black pepper

Melt the margarine and gently fry the finely chopped onion and garlic for a few minutes. Add the peeled, or well-scrubbed, sliced artichokes and stir well. Pour in stock, adding the bouquet garni, nutmeg and seasoning. Simmer until tender, remove bouquet, add juice and nutmeg. Blend cornflour with a little water and add. Boil for 2 minutes, check seasoning and serve.

MARROW CASSEROLE

1 small marrow
2 large onions
6 tomatoes

salt and black pepper
1 oz (30g) margarine

Slice onions and the skinned tomatoes, place half in a greased ovenproof dish and season. Top with the marrow cut in rings, ½-inch thick, then the rest of the onions and tomatoes and more seasoning. Dot with margarine, cover and bake for about 1 hour at 375°F — Mark 5.

MUSHROOM SURPRISE

12 oz (340g) mushrooms
1 large green pepper
1 onion
¼ pint (150ml) grape juice
   (red if possible)
2 tablespoons French mustard
2 tablespoons brown sugar

2 tablespoons Holbrook's
   Worcestershire sauce
3 tablespoons olive oil
1 tablespoon tarragon
   vinegar
salt and black pepper

Peel and chop the onion and fry it gently in the oil for a few minutes. Add the sliced mushrooms and peppers and fry for another 5 minutes, stirring. Mix all the other ingredients together and add to the mushrooms. Simmer gently for about 40 minutes or until the peppers are tender and the sauce thick.

NUTTY CELERY

1 head of celery
3 oz (90g) almonds or
  cashews
1 teaspoon paprika

1 teaspoon chopped
  parsley
1 oz (30g) margarine

Wash the celery well, cut into 2-inch pieces and keep the leaves if fresh-looking. Cook the celery in boiling, salted water until tender. Heat the margarine, add the paprika and nuts and fry quickly until browned. Add the parsley and sprinkle this mixture over the drained celery and serve at once. If the celery leaves are fresh, chop them up and add them with the parsley.

ONION AND POTATO CASSEROLE

1 lb (450g) new potatoes
12 oz (340g) button onions
1 oz (30g) margarine
1 teaspoon brown sugar

1 tablespoon chopped
  parsley
½ pint (300ml) stock
seasoning

Peel the onions and plunge them in boiling water for a minute, drain them and place them, in a flameproof casserole if possible, with the margarine, sugar, stock and seasoning. Boil until the onions are tender and there is just a little liquid left.

Scrape the potatoes and cook in boiling salted water and drain. Add them to the onions with the parsley, and serve straight from the casserole.

PAN–FRIED POTATOES

1 lb (450g) potatoes
1 onion
salt and black pepper

2 tablespoons chopped
  parsley
plenty of oil for frying

1 oz (30g) gram flour (see   1 oz (30g) plain flour
  p. 132)

Peel and grate potatoes and onion. Stir in parsley and seasoning.
Sift the flours and stir to a fairly thick batter with cold water. Stir
into the potato mixture.

    Heat oil in large pan, pour in the potato mixture, reduce heat
and cook for about 15 minutes on each side until cooked through
and brown. Serve hot.

PEAS WITH MUSHROOMS

1 lb (450g) peas   1 tablespoon chopped
4 oz (120g) mushrooms   chives
2 oz (60g) margarine $\frac{1}{2}$ teaspoon brown sugar
$\frac{1}{2}$ teaspoon salt

Cook the peas in $\frac{1}{2}$ pint (300 ml) water with the sugar and salt until
tender. Heat the margarine and fry the sliced mushrooms for a few
minutes. Add the drained peas and stir in the chives. Serve hot.

PEAS WITH NUTS

1 lb (450g) peas $\frac{1}{2}$ teaspoon brown sugar
3 oz (90g) shelled peanuts $\frac{1}{2}$ teaspoon salt
  or hazelnuts   1 tablespoon chopped
1 oz (30g) margarine   parsley
$\frac{1}{2}$ teaspoon chilli powder

Cook the peas in $\frac{1}{2}$ pint (300 ml) water with the sugar and salt until
tender. Melt the margarine, add the chilli powder and nuts and fry
quickly until browned. Add the drained peas and serve garnished
with the parsley.

PETITS POIS

$1\frac{1}{2}$ lb (670g) fresh young peas   1 teaspoon brown sugar
1 bunch spring onions   1 heaped teaspoon
1 lettuce heart   cornflour
1 oz (30g) margarine   salt and black pepper

Put trimmed onions, shredded lettuce and shelled peas in pan with the sugar, seasoning, margarine and 4 tablespoons water. Cover and simmer until peas are tender. Blend the cornflour with 3 tablespoons water and stir it in. Boil for a minute, check seasoning and serve.

POTATO AND ONION FRITTERS

1 lb (450g) potatoes
2 tablespoons Smokey
   Snaps (see p. 133,
   optional)

1 onion
2 tablespoons flour
salt and black pepper
plenty of oil for frying

Peel potatoes and onion and grate both on fairly coarse grater. Mix with the Smokey Snaps, seasoning and flour. Fry tablespoons of the mixture in the oil until brown on both sides. Flatten the mixture in the pan and cook fairly slowly so that the potato cooks right through.

POTATOES AND MUSHROOMS

1 lb (450g) potatoes
8 oz (230g) mushrooms
1 oz (30g) margarine
3 tablespoons olive oil
1 onion

1 clove of garlic
1 tablespoon lemon juice
1 tablespoon chopped
   parsley
salt and black pepper

Heat the oil and margarine and gently fry the finely chopped onion and garlic for a few minutes. Add the potatoes, peeled and thinly sliced, and continue to cook slowly. After a few minutes add the sliced mushrooms, seasoning and enough water to just cover.

Simmer slowly until potatoes are tender, add the juice and parsley, check seasoning and serve.

PUREED AUBERGINES

2 aubergines
1 onion
1 clove of garlic
3 tomatoes

1 teaspoon coriander
   powder
$\frac{1}{2}$ teaspoon chilli powder
$\frac{1}{2}$ teaspoon turmeric

½ teaspoon cumin powder
salt and black pepper
3 tablespoons oil or ghee

fresh coriander leaves or
parsley

Place the aubergines in a hot oven or grill until the skin turns black. Remove the skin and mash the flesh. Fry the onion and tomatoes gently in the oil for a few minutes. Add the spices and fry for a couple of minutes.

Stir in the aubergine flesh, season and continue to cook slowly for 5-10 minutes. Serve garnished with the coriander leaves.

PUREED SPROUTS

1 lb (450g) sprouts
4 tablespoons thick soya
  milk

1 oz (30g) margarine
¼ teaspoon nutmeg
salt and black pepper

Cook sprouts in boiling salted water until nearly tender. Liquidize with the milk and reheat with the margarine, seasoning and nutmeg.

RED CABBAGE

1½ lb (670g) red cabbage
1 onion
1 cooking apple
2 tablespoons lemon juice
1 tablespoon brown sugar
1 teaspoon salt
2 teaspoons cornflour

3 cloves
½-inch cinnamon stick
1 bay leaf
¾ pint (400ml) water or
stock
2 tablespoons oil

Wash and shred the cabbage and cook gently in the oil for a couple of minutes. Add the peeled onion with the cloves stuck in it, the juice, cinnamon and bay leaf. Continue to cook gently for 10 minutes.

Add the diced apple, sugar, salt and water and simmer, stirring occasionally, until tender. Remove the onion and cinnamon stick and bay leaf.

Blend the cornflour with a little cold water and stir it in. Simmer for another 2 minutes, stirring well. Check seasoning and serve.

RED POTATOES

1 lb (450g) potatoes
5 tablespoons tomato
 purée
3 tablespoons olive oil

8 stoned black olives
2 oz (60g) breadcrumbs
2 bay leaves
salt and black pepper

Warm the oil in a shallow pan, add the purée and the potatoes, peeled and cut in fairly thin slices. Cook gently for a few minutes, then add the bay leaves, seasoning and enough water to just cover the potatoes. Simmer for about 30 minutes or until potatoes are just tender.

Place in an ovenproof dish with the olives, cover with crumbs and bake at 325°F — Mark 3 for 30 minutes.

SICILIAN AUBERGINE

1 aubergine
2 sticks of celery
6 tomatoes
1 teaspoon brown sugar
2 teaspoons capers

1 tablespoon chopped
 fresh mint
1 teaspoon salt
pinch cayenne
4 tablespoons olive oil

Dice the aubergine and celery and fry in half the oil. In another pan fry the peeled, chopped tomatoes in the rest of the oil, adding the sugar, salt and cayenne. When the tomatoes have made a thick sauce, stir in the fried vegetables, mint and capers. Check seasoning and serve.

SMOKEY CAULIFLOWER

1 large cauliflower
1 onion
1 clove of garlic
1 tablespoon lemon juice
2 oz (60g) margarine
1 tablespoon Smokey
 Snaps (see p. 133)

2 tablespoons oil
3 tablespoons
 breadcrumbs
1 tablespoon chopped
 parsley
salt and black pepper

Wash cauliflower well and break into small florets and cook in boiling salted water for a couple of minutes until just tender. Drain.

Heat the oil and margarine together and gently fry the finely chopped onion and garlic for a few minutes. Add the rest of the ingredients, mix well.

Place cauliflower in a shallow greased ovenproof dish, cover with crumb mixture and bake for 15 minutes at 375°F — Mark 5, basting once in its own juice.

SMOKEY TOMATOES

1 lb (450g) tomatoes
1 large onion
2 tablespoons Smokey
  Snaps (see p. 133)
4 large slices wholemeal
  bread, crumbed

1 oz (30g) margarine
1 tablespoon chopped
  parsley
½ teaspoon basil
salt and black pepper

Skin and slice the tomatoes. Mix the crumbs, herbs, Smokey Snaps and seasoning. In a greased ovenproof dish place alternate layers of tomato and the crumb mixture, ending with a layer of crumbs. Dot with the margarine and bake at 400°F — Mark 6 for 30 minutes.

SPROUT SPECIAL

1 lb (450g) small sprouts
8 oz (230g) seedless grapes
2 oz (60g) margarine

½ pint (300ml) white grape
  juice
salt and pepper

Prepare sprouts and cook until tender in the grape juice. Drain (adding juice to stockpot). Add the margarine, grapes and seasoning, stir gently until well mixed and serve at once.

STIR–FRY SPINACH

1½ lb (670g) spinach
1 onion
2 cloves of garlic
1 teaspoon ginger, minced

1 teaspoon sugar
1 teaspoon salt
2 tablespoons soy sauce
3 tablespoons oil

Wash the spinach well and remove the tough stalks. Tear the larger leaves in thirds. Peel and mince the onion and garlic, and fry in very hot oil in a large frying pan with the minced ginger.

After a minute, add the spinach and salt, and continue cooking on high heat for a couple of minutes, stirring well. Add the soy sauce and sugar and cook on a lower heat for about three minutes more.

Serve at once. For special occasions, a little wine or sherry can be added at the final stage.

STIR-FRY TOMATOES

6 tomatoes
2 spring onions
2 cloves of garlic
½ small cucumber
1 teaspoon minced ginger
2 teaspoons Miso (see
  p. 133)

3 tablespoons soy sauce
2 teaspoons sugar
salt to taste
4 tablespoons oil

Skin and quarter the tomatoes, cut the unpeeled cucumber into strips. Chop the whole spring onions and crush the garlic. Fry the onions, garlic and ginger in the hot oil in a large frying pan. After half a minute add the cucumber and continue to stir-fry for another minute or so.

Stir in the tomatoes, sugar, Miso and soy sauce and cook for another three minute. Serve at once.

STIR-FRY VEGETABLES

1 onion
1 clove of garlic
2 sticks of celery
½ white cabbage

1 carrot
1 teaspoon minced ginger
½ teaspoon salt
3 tablespoons oil

Heat the oil and fry the minced garlic and ginger for a few moments. Add the sliced onion, celery and carrot, cut in thin strips. Fry over high heat for one minute. Add the finely shredded cabbage and salt. Cover and cook for 4 minutes, stirring occasionally. Serve at once.

STUFFED TOMATOES

4 large tomatoes
2 thick slices of bread
2 tablespoons chopped
  parsley

2 tablespoons olive oil
salt and black pepper
1 teaspoon lemon juice
1 clove of garlic

Halve the tomatoes, scoop out juice and leave upside down to drain. Rub bread with garlic on both sides, moisten it with oil and leave to soften. When soft, crumble it, adding the juice, parsley and seasoning.

Stuff the tomatoes with this mixture, brush surface with oil and place under a slow grill. Turn the grill up after a few minutes to brown the tops. Serve at once, perhaps in a bed of watercress.

SULTANA SPINACH

$1\frac{1}{2}$ lb (670g) spinach
1 oz (30g) sultanas
1 oz (30g) broken cashew
  nuts

1 clove of garlic
1 oz (30g) margarine
1 tablespoon olive oil
salt and black pepper

Wash the spinach well and cook with no extra water but a little salt until tender. Drain and press the liquid out of it (into the stockpot of course). Warm the oil and margarine in a large pan, add the minced garlic, spinach and pepper. Mix well, then add the sultanas and nuts. Cover and cook gently for 10 minutes.

SWEET AND SOUR COURGETTES

1 lb (450g) courgettes
2 tablespoons cider
  vinegar
1 tablespoon brown sugar

2 tablespoons olive oil
$\frac{1}{4}$ teaspoon cinnamon
salt and black pepper

Slice courgettes, sprinkle with salt and leave for 30 minutes at least. Wipe them dry and fry gently in the oil. When nearly done add all the other ingredients, cook a few minutes more and serve.

TURNIPS WITH GARLIC

1 lb (450g) turnips
2 tablespoons olive oil
3 cloves of garlic
2 teaspoons lemon juice

1 tablespoon chopped
  parsley
salt and black pepper

Peel the turnips and cook in boiling salted water for 5 minutes. Drain and cut into quarters. Heat the oil in a large pan, add the turnips and seasoning and fry gently until cooked. Add the crushed garlic, lemon juice and parsley and serve.

Salads

Salads should be eaten as often as possible. Nearly all vegetables are more nutritious eaten raw. In fact it is both possible and healthy to live without any cooked food, with the exception of, perhaps, wholemeal bread and cereals. A diet of fresh vegetables, fruit, nuts and bean, lentil or grain sprouts, moistened with French dressing and eaten with wholemeal bread and margarine should supply all your nutritional requirements (with the exception of vitamin B12 — see p. 26).

The basic French dressing can be varied in many ways. You can use different types of vinegar, add a little chilli powder or a spoonful of fresh herbs. All sorts of combinations are possible with salads. You may well have your favourite recipes already. The recipes in this section are only a guide, which you can vary and extend as your imagination expands.

Bean sprouts are very high in nutritional value and can be bought from Chinese shops. It is, however, easy to make your own. Place 1 oz (30g) moong or aduki beans in a clean jam jar. Fill with warm water and leave overnight. Tie a piece of muslin or clean cloth over the jar and secure with a rubber band. Strain out the water, fill with cold water and strain again. Dry the muslin, tip the jar on its side to drain and leave in a dark place. Continue to rinse out three times a day for 3-5 days, or until well sprouted. As they will increase in bulk considerably, do not use too many beans to start with or you will have an overflow problem! Other beans and grains can be sprouted, e.g. alfalfa, wheat grain, soya beans. You can buy small quantities of seed for sprouting from seed merchants such as Thompson and Morgan, or from your health food shop. However it is far cheaper to buy moong beans in bulk and use a couple of spoonfuls for sprouting whenever you want to.

BLACK-EYED BEAN SALAD

6 oz (180g) black-eyed beans	2 tablespoons chopped parsley
2 onions	French dressing (p. 92)
salt and black pepper	1 tablespoon lemon juice

Soak the beans overnight and cook in plenty of water until just tender. Drain. While still hot add the parsley, finely chopped onions, juice, dressing and seasoning to taste.

BROAD BEAN SALAD

8 oz (230g) broad beans	2 teaspoons chopped parsley
2 bunches watercress	French dressing (p. 92)
1 small onion	
salt and black pepper	

Cook the beans in boiling water until tender. Drain. Wash the watercress well and place in bowl. Mix finely sliced onion with the beans and dressing. Season, place on watercress and garnish with parsley.

CELERY, APPLE AND BEETROOT SALAD

4 sticks of celery
2 small, cooked beetroot

3 crisp eating apples
Vegan Mayonnaise (p. 92)

Clean celery and leave it to soak in cold, salted water to crisp it. Peel and chop the beetroot, cut the apple up but do not peel it, then chop the celery into ½-inch lengths. Combine all the vegetables and add enough mayonnaise to coat them. The mayonnaise should take on a pretty pink colour from the beetroot.

CHICK-PEA SALAD

6 oz (180g) chick-peas
3 oz (90g) nuts
4 tablespoons
  breadcrumbs
2 tablespoons lemon juice
1 clove of garlic

½ pint (300ml) stock
½ teaspoon chilli powder
salt and black pepper
1 tablespoon chopped
  parsley

Soak chick-peas overnight and boil in plenty of water until tender. Drain. Liquidize the nuts and garlic, adding a little stock if necessary. Add the rest of the stock, the crumbs, juice, chilli powder and seasoning and mix well until a creamy consistency. Stir in the chick-peas and garnish with parsley.

CHICORY, ORANGE AND WATERCRESS SALAD

2 heads of chicory
1 bunch of watercress

2 oranges
French dressing (p. 92)

Peel oranges carefully, slice in thick rounds and quarter each round. Remove outer layers of chicory and slice. Wash watercress well and remove tough stalks. Combine all the vegetables in a bowl and toss in dressing before serving.

COLESLAW

½ large white cabbage
3 carrots
1 small green pepper
2 small onions

1 tablespoon tomato purée
1 teaspoon brown sugar
French dressing (p. 92)

Wash the cabbage and shred finely, scrape and grate the carrots on a coarse grater and chop the pepper and onions finely. Mix the purée and sugar with the dressing. Combine all the vegetables in a bowl and toss well in the dressing.

COLOURFUL CABBAGE SALAD

½ large red or white
  cabbage
4 oz (120g) dried apricots
4 tablespoons orange juice

2 oz (60g) walnuts
1 orange
1 small carrot
French dressing (p. 92)

Wash the cabbage and shred finely. Soak the apricots in the orange juice, then chop them. Peel the orange and divide in segments. Grate the carrot coarsely. Combine all the ingredients and moisten well with dressing.

CONTINENTAL SALAD

2 small aubergines
2 green peppers
1 onion
1 clove of garlic
8 oz (230g) French beans,
  cooked
4 oz (120g) button
  mushrooms

3 tomatoes
1 teaspoon marjoram
1 tablespoon chopped
  parsley
salt and black pepper
2 tablespoons oil
6 stoned black olives
French dressing (p. 92)

Slice aubergines, sprinkle with salt and leave for 30 minutes. Wipe dry and fry in oil until tender. Chop the onion and peppers finely. Rub bowl with garlic and in it mix the aubergines, onion, peppers, sliced beans, mushrooms, olives, marjoram, seasoning and plenty of dressing.

Leave overnight or for several hours. Add skinned, chopped tomatoes and parsley before serving.

DANDELION SALAD

enough dandelion leaves
  for 4
2 slices bread
1 clove of garlic

3 tablespoons oil
1 tablespoon Smokey
  Snaps (see p. 133,
  optional)

Choose young leaves and wash them well. Halve the garlic and rub it on both sides of the bread. Cut the bread into small cubes and fry quickly in hot oil until brown and crisp. Place the leaves in a bowl, mix the Smokey Snaps with the croûtons of bread and heap them up in the centre. Serve at once.

FAMILY SALAD

8 oz (230g) white cabbage
1 carrot
2 crisp eating apples
3 tablespoons sultanas

3 tablespoons salted
  peanuts
1 teaspoon brown sugar
French dressing (p. 92)

Wash and shred the cabbage finely and grate the carrot coarsely. Cut the unpeeled apples in strips. Combine cabbage, carrot, apples, nuts and sultanas. Mix sugar with dressing and add to salad just before serving, tossing well.

FLAMING SALAD

4 tomatoes
2 oranges
4 spring onions

8 stoned black olives
French dressing (p. 92)

Peel oranges carefully and slice into rounds. Cut tomatoes into rounds and place in a shallow dish, overlapping alternate slices of tomato and orange. Chop the onions and olives finely and sprinkle on top. Trickle the dressing over all.

HOT TOMATO SALAD

4 large tomatoes
1 large onion

2 green chillies
salt and sugar to taste

Scald and skin the tomatoes and mash or liquidize. Chop the

chillies very finely and grate the onion. Combine all the vegetables and add salt and sugar.

LEEK AND CELERY SALAD

2 small leeks
1 small head of celery
3 tablespoons orange juice

1 tablespoon chopped
  chives or parsley

Wash the celery and leave to soak in cold, salted water to crisp it. Dry and cut in ½-inch slices. Cut off the darkest part of the leek leaves (for the stockpot) and slice the leeks into very thin slices. Combine the vegetables with the orange juice and chives.

LEEK SALAD

3 small leeks
2 tablespoons lemon juice
1 heaped teaspoon
  cornflour

1 tablespoon olive oil
2 teaspoons chopped
  parsley
salt and black pepper

Remove darkest green leaves from leeks. Slice the leeks and cook until tender in boiling, salted water. Drain, leaving just enough water to cover them. Mix the cornflour with a little cold water and stir into the remaining leek water. Bring to the boil, cool and add juice, oil and seasoning to taste. Serve cold, garnished with the parsley.

LETTUCE AND COURGETTE SALAD

1 large head lettuce
1 bunch watercress

3 courgettes
French dressing (p. 92)

Cut the courgettes in fairly thin slices and cook in boiling salted water until just tender. Drain and place in a bowl of cold water for a few minutes. Wash and dry the lettuce and watercress.

Arrange broken lettuce leaves around sides and bottom of salad bowl, place the drained courgette slices in a layer and top with the watercress. Pour on French dressing just before serving.

NUT COLESLAW

1 small white cabbage
2 red-skinned apples
4 oz (120g) salted cashew
  or peanuts

½ cucumber
a little salt
about 4 fl. oz (150ml)
  Vegan Mayonnaise (see
  p. 92)

Shred the cabbage and dice the cucumber and apple. Mix all the ingredients together and serve.

NUTTY ORANGE SALAD

3 oranges
2 oz (60g) nuts
1 lettuce

2 teaspoons chopped
  parsley
French dressing (p. 92)

Wash and dry lettuce and place in bowl. Peel and slice the oranges and chop the nuts. Place oranges on lettuce, top with nuts. Add dressing and garnish with parsley.

NUTTY RICE SALAD

6 oz (180g) rice
2 oz (60g) currants
2 oz (60g) chopped nuts

salt and black pepper
French dressing (p. 92)

Cook rice in boiling salted water, drain well. While still warm add the currants, nuts, dressing and seasoning to taste.

ORANGE AND CUCUMBER SALAD

2 oranges
½ large cucumber
4 spring onions

1 round lettuce
French dressing (p. 92)

Chop the onions very finely. Peel the oranges and cut in thin slices. Wash the cucumber and cut into wafer-thin slices. Wash and dry lettuce and arrange in bottom of bowl. Combine the other vegetables and pile up in centre. Add dressing just before serving.

ORANGE RICE SALAD

6 oz (180g) rice
1 orange
2 oz (60g) currants

salt and black pepper
French dressing (p. 92)

Wash the orange well in hot water, dry, and grate the rind finely. Add 1 tablespoon of the juice to the dressing. Cook the rice in boiling, salted water, adding the rind 5 minutes before the end of cooking time. Drain. While still warm add the currants, dressing and seasoning to taste.

PEPPER AND ONION SALAD

2 large onions
1 green pepper
2 oranges

8 stoned black olives
$\frac{1}{2}$ teaspoon brown sugar
French dressing (p. 92)

Slice the onions very thinly. Peel the oranges and cut into thin slices. Cut the pepper into rings. Add the sugar to the dressing. Mix all the ingredients, moistening well with dressing.

POTATO SALAD

1 lb (450g) potatoes
2 tablespoons chopped
  chives
1 lettuce

1 tablespoon chopped
  parsley
French dressing (p. 92)

Peel the potatoes, chop fairly small and cook in boiling, salted water for about 5 minutes or until just tender. Drain. While still warm add the herbs and enough dressing to moisten well. Cool and serve on a bed of lettuce.

RICE SALAD

4 oz (120g) rice
3 tomatoes
4 oz (120g) button
  mushrooms
1 tablespoon oil

2 tablespoons stoned
  black olives
French dressing (p. 92)
parsley

Boil the rice in salted water and drain. While still warm add the chopped, skinned tomatoes, the olives and the mushrooms lightly fried in the oil. Add enough dressing to moisten well and garnish with chopped parsley.

SALAD PLATTER

4 oz (120g) green grapes
4 oz (120g) black grapes
2 oranges
3 tomatoes
½ cucumber

½ green pepper
½ bunch spring onions
2 oz (60g) raisins
2 oz (60g) chopped nuts
French dressing (p. 92)

Peel the oranges and separate into segments. Quarter the tomatoes, slice the cucumber and dice the pepper. Chop the spring onions finely. Arrange all the fruit and vegetables in rows on a long plate. Sprinkle the nuts and raisins on top and trickle on the dressing just before serving.

SPICE AND RICE SALAD

6 oz (180g) rice
1-inch piece ginger
1 oz (30g) raisins
4 dried apricots
2 spring onions
1 oz (30g) pine nuts

½ teaspoon coriander
 powder
¼ teaspoon nutmeg
salt and black pepper
French dressing (p. 92)

Peel the ginger and place in water in which the rice is cooking. Drain rice and remove ginger. Soak the apricots and cook lightly with the raisins. While the rice is still warm gently stir in the seasoning, spices, finely chopped onions and apricots, the raisins and dressing. Use the nuts as a garnish.

SURPRISE POTATO SALAD

1 lb (450g) potatoes
3 crisp eating apples
1 tablespoon chopped
  chives

1 tablespoon capers
salt and black pepper
French dressing (p. 92)

Peel potatoes and cut in fairly small pieces. Cook in boiling salted water for 5 minutes or until tender. Drain. Chop the apples and mix with the potatoes, adding the capers, chives, dressing and seasoning.

FRENCH DRESSING

6 tablespoons olive oil
3 tablespoons lemon juice
  or vinegar and lemon
  juice

1 clove of garlic
1 bay leaf
salt and black pepper

Combine all the ingredients in a screw-top jar and shake vigorously. You can mix them in your blender if you prefer. It is best to make this dressing some time before serving, to let the flavour of the garlic and bay leaf develop. The flavour can also be varied by using different flavoured vinegars, or by adding a little mustard. You can keep this dressing indefinitely, simply changing the garlic clove and bay leaf every week or so.

VEGAN MAYONNAISE

3 tablespoons Plamil (see
  p. 133)
3 tablespoons oil

3 tablespoons lemon juice
1 teaspoon brown sugar
salt to taste

Whisk all the ingredients, in the blender if you have one. Add the juice last. Add finely chopped chives, parsley or any fresh herb before serving. This dressing keeps for three days in the fridge if covered. For variety, try adding a little mustard or curry powder, or some tomato purée.

You can make a similar mayonnaise using Granogen. This will keep for longer in the fridge.

Puddings

I have tried to include a wide variety of puddings in this section. Many adults have already developed a sweet tooth and children usually feel a meal is not complete without a pudding. However these puddings are all of nutritional value in their own right. It is up to the cook to achieve a sensible balance, serving a light fruit dish after a heavy main course or a cereal-based pudding after a vegetable-based main dish.

It is worth remembering that favourite milk dishes can still be made, using soya milk or diluted plant milk. It is best to use barbados or muscovado sugar as white sugar is often bleached over fires of bone charcoal. Molasses can be used instead of sugar, if you can get used to its very strong flavour. If you have any favourite recipes which are vegan but for their gelatine content, you can substitute agar-agar at the rate of $\frac{1}{2}$ oz (15g) agar-agar for 2 oz (60g) gelatine for 2 pints (1 litre) liquid. Agar-agar is sprinkled over hot liquid and stirred in very quickly.

It is sensible to try to reduce your sugar intake. Rather than cut out sugar completely, you can gradually reduce the amount used in drinks and puddings. Strict vegans do not use honey, believing it to be the property of the bees. Modern bee-keeping also can involve artificial stimulants to production, which may necessitate exploitation of the bees.

I have included a recipe for Nut Cream at the end of this section (p. 111). It makes a delicious alternative to real cream. However you can also make up some Granogen, using more powder and less water than usual to get a thick consistency. You can also buy the thick version of Plamil, which is called Delice.

APPLE CRUMBLE

6 oz (180g) wholemeal or
  81% flour
4 oz (120g) margarine or
  oil
3 oz (90g) sugar
3 large cooking apples

2 tablespoons brown
  sugar
3 cloves
$\frac{1}{4}$ teaspoon cinnamon
$\frac{1}{4}$ teaspoon nutmeg

Peel, core and chop apples coarsely. Place in pan with the brown sugar, spices and a very little water. Cook very gently for 3 minutes and place in an ovenproof dish. Melt the margarine and stir into the flour and sugar. Mix well until a crumbly texture forms. Place on top of apples and bake at 350°F — Mark 4 for about 40 minutes or until browning well.

APPLE CRUNCH

4 oz (120g) porridge oats
2 oz (60g) wholemeal flour
2 oz (60g) broken cashew
  nuts
2 tablespoons brown
  sugar
3 oz (90g) margarine

3 large cooking apples
2 tablespoons brown
  sugar
3 cloves
$\frac{1}{4}$ teaspoon cinnamon
$\frac{1}{4}$ teaspoon nutmeg

Cook the last five ingredients for a few minutes with a little water, having peeled and sliced the apples first. Place in a greased ovenproof dish. Put the first four ingredients in a bowl and stir in the melted margarine. When well mixed, place on top of the apples. Bake at 350°F — Mark 4 for 30-40 minutes or until well browned.

APPLE PASTIES

8 oz (230g) 81% plain
  flour
4 oz (120g) margarine
½ teaspoon salt
½ teaspoon sugar
lemon juice and water to
  bind

Filling:
2 cooking apples
1 oz (30g) sultanas
2 tablespoons brown
  sugar
little powdered
  cinnamon, nutmeg and
  clove

Rub margarine into flour, salt and sugar. Make into dough with juice and water and roll out on floured board to ¼-inch thickness. Cut into 5-inch rounds. Place some peeled, chopped apple, sugar, sultanas and spice on each round, leaving half the round empty.

Fold this side over the filling and seal the edges with a wet finger. Make slits in the top for steam to escape. Place on greased baking sheet and bake at 425°F — Mark 7 for 10 minutes, then at 375°F — Mark 5 for about 20 minutes. Delicious hot or cold with Delice or Nut Cream (p. 111).

APPLE STICKJAW

1 lb (450g) cooking apples
2 oz (60g) flaked tapioca
2 oz (60g) brown sugar

3 cloves
½ oz (15g) margarine

Place tapioca in bowl, cover with cold water and leave for 30 minutes at least. Peel and chop apples and stew gently for a few minutes with the sugar, cloves and a little water. Stir into the tapioca, place in greased ovenproof dish and dot with the margarine. Cover and bake at 350°F — Mark 4 for 1 hour.

Served hot, this will be runny and will go well with Nut Cream (see p. 111). Served cold, it solidifies, but some people prefer it that way. This pudding can also be made with rhubarb.

APRICOT ALMOND FLAN

Pastry:

8 oz (230g) 81% plain flour
2 oz (60g) ground almonds
5 oz (150g) margarine
1 tablespoon sugar,
    ground fine
lemon juice and water to
    bind

Filling:

½ pint (300ml) soya milk
2 oz (60g) ground almonds
1 oz (30g) sugar
1 tablespoon cornflour
½ teaspoon almond essence
2 bananas
1 can apricots

To make pastry, rub margarine into dry ingredients, bind with juice and water and roll out to line a flan tin. Bake blind at 375°F— Mark 5 for 30 minutes or until golden. Cool in tin, then place on serving plate.

For the filling, blend cornflour and soya milk and bring to the boil, stirring. Simmer for 2 minutes, then whisk in the sugar, almonds and essence. Pour onto flan and cool. Place the apricots and sliced bananas on top, spreading a little of the syrup from the can on top of the fruit.

APRICOT WATER ICE

8 oz (230g) fresh apricots
4 oz (120g) sugar

1 orange
1 lemon

Place sugar in pan with ½ pint (300ml) water and heat slowly until sugar dissolves. Boil for about 10 minutes. Meanwhile, wash and stone the apricots, and liquidize them thoroughly, adding the juices of the orange and lemon. When syrup is ready, stir in the fruit purée and mix well.

Pour into shallow dish and place in freezer compartment of fridge at coldest setting. After an hour or so remove and beat. Return to fridge until frozen.

BAKED APPLES WITH MINCEMEAT

4 large cooking apples
4 tablespoons vegan
    mincemeat

4 teaspoons brown sugar
1 oz (30g) margarine

Wash and core the apples and place in a greased ovenproof dish. Score each one at the centre to prevent skins splitting. Place a spoonful of the mincemeat in the cavity of each apple, top with a teaspoon of sugar and a knob of margarine. Bake at 375°F — Mark 5 for about 30-40 minutes.

(Vegan mincemeat can be obtained from Health Food Stores. Vegetable fat is used instead of suet.)

BAKED BANANAS

4 large or 6 medium
 bananas
2 oz (60g) brown sugar

2 oz (60g) margarine
2 tablespoons lemon juice

Peel and slice bananas in half, lengthways. Place in a shallow ovenproof dish, greased. Cover with the juice, sugar and melted margarine. Bake at 350°F — Mark 4 for about 25 minutes. Serve hot with Nut Cream (p. 111).

BAKED FRUIT PUDDING

6 oz (180g) 81% flour
2 oz (60g) brown sugar
2 oz (60g) margarine
¼ pint (150ml) soya milk
2 teaspoons cornflour

2 teaspoons baking
 powder
2 oz (60g) sultanas
1 oz (30g) currants

Place flour, cornflour and baking powder in bowl. Gently heat the milk, sugar and margarine until well blended. Cool and stir into the dry ingredients. Add the fruit and check that consistency is moist enough; it should be fairly stiff.

Place in a greased ovenproof bowl and bake at 375°F — Mark 5 for 45-50 minutes. Turn out and serve with vegan custard or a fruit purée. Vegan custard is easily made. Use your normal custard powder but add soya milk instead of cow's milk.

BAKED STUFFED PEACHES

4 large peaches
2 oz (60g) ground almonds

2 oz (60g) soft brown
 breadcrumbs

2 oz (60g) brown sugar
2 tablespoons mincemeat
  (vegan)

1 oz (30g) margarine
$\frac{1}{4}$ teaspoon cinnamon

Skin, halve and stone the peaches. Place them in a greased ovenproof dish. Mix all the other ingredients and stuff the peach cavities, scooping out a little flesh if necessary. Bake at 350°F — Mark 4 for about 30 minutes. Serve hot.

BAKEWELL TART

Pastry:
6 oz (180g) 81% plain
  flour
3 oz (90g) margarine
$\frac{1}{2}$ teaspoon salt
1 teaspoon sugar
lemon juice and water to
  mix

Filling:
3 tablespoons raspberry
  jam
3 oz (90g) margarine
3 oz (90g) brown sugar
3 oz (90g) cake or soft
  breadcrumbs
1 teaspoon almond
  essence

Rub margarine into dry ingredients and bind to a stiff dough with juice and water. Roll out on floured board and line a greased pie dish with the pastry. Prick pastry with fork and spread with jam. Mix the other ingredients well and spread on top of jam. Bake at 375°F — Mark 5 for 40 minutes or until golden brown.

BANANA ICE-CREAM SPECIAL

3 bananas
2 tablespoons brown
  sugar
6 tablespoons orange juice

2 tablespoons lemon juice
1 can Delice cream
2 oz (60g) chopped
  roasted almonds

Liquidize or mash the bananas with the juices and sugar. Stir in the cream and freeze until set. Return to bowl and whisk well. Stir in the almonds and freeze until completely set.

BANANA WHIP

4 bananas
1 tablespoon lemon juice

1 orange
4 oz (120g) brown sugar
8 oz (230g) Nut Cream

1 teaspoon agar-agar
4 tablespoons water

Mash the bananas and add the lemon juice and rind and juice of the orange. Dissolve the sugar in the water over low heat, then bring to the boil and sprinkle on the agar-agar and stir well until it has dissolved. Add to the banana mixture and finally stir in the Nut Cream (see p. 111). Chill before serving.

CARAMEL ORANGES

4 oranges
6 oz (180g) demerara sugar

4 fl. oz (140ml) water

Peel rind from 2 oranges thinly and cut into matchstick shapes. Peel remaining oranges and be careful to remove pith from al! four oranges. Place sugar and water in a heavy pan, heat gently until sugar has dissolved, then boil until thick, about 8 minutes. Add the peeled oranges, reduce heat, and gently turn the oranges over in the syrup for a couple of minutes. Place oranges on serving dish.

Meanwhile boil the strips of rind for 7 minutes, drain them and add to the syrup, heating until they start to look transparent and caramelized. Don't let them turn into toffee. Place a spoonful of the rind on top of each orange. Serve cold.

CASSATA

4 large, ripe bananas
1 oz (30g) chopped nuts
1 oz (30g) currants

1 oz (30g) finely chopped
dates or dried apricots

Liquidize or mash the bananas and add the other ingredients. Place in freezer compartment of fridge, which should be at coldest setting. If possible, beat the cassata after an hour or so and return it to the fridge until fully frozen. For variety, leave out the dates and grate in a little dark chocolate.

CHOCOLATE BLANCMANGE

1 pint (550ml) soya milk

2 tablespoons cornflour

1½ tablespoons cocoa   2 tablespoons sugar
   powder

Blend all the dry ingredients with a little milk. Heat the rest of the milk. When nearly boiling, pour onto the chocolate mixture, stir well and return to pan. Boil gently for a minute, stirring all the time. Serve hot or cold.

CHOCOLATE ICE-CREAM

1 tablespoon cocoa   4 large, ripe bananas
   powder   6 oz (180g) ground cashew
2 tablespoons brown   nuts
   sugar

Liquidize the bananas. Mix the cocoa and sugar with a tablespoon of water and add to the bananas. Finally add the nuts and blend well. Place in freezer compartment of fridge at coldest setting and freeze for several hours. Instant coffee powder may be used instead, or carob powder, which won't require any sugar.

CHOCOLATE SURPRISE PUDDING

8 oz (230g) dark chocolate   3 oz (90g) wholemeal
   (Terry's Bitter is vegan)   breadcrumbs
1 pint (550ml) soya milk   1 oz (30g) margarine
1 tablespoon cornflour   2 tablespoons sharp jam,
½ teaspoon vanilla essence   e.g. raspberry

Melt margarine and stir into crumbs and jam. Place this mixture in a serving dish. Dissolve the chocolate in the milk over very gentle heat. Blend the cornflour with a little milk.

When the chocolate has dissolved, stir into the cornflour then return to pan. Boil gently for a couple of minutes, stirring all the time. Add essence. Cool and pour over crumb mixture. Serve cold.

CHRISTMAS PUDDING

1 lb (450g) raisins (use half   8 oz (230g) sultanas
   Muscatel if you can)   8 oz (230g) currants

1 cooking apple
2 carrots
8 oz (230g) Suenut
8 oz (230g) brown sugar
6 oz (340g) wholemeal
   breadcrumbs
4 oz (120g) wholemeal
   flour

1 lemon
2 oz (60g) chopped
   almonds
$\frac{1}{4}$ teaspoon nutmeg
1 teaspoon mixed spice
$\frac{1}{2}$ pint (300ml) orange juice
   (or whisky and orange
   juice, mixed)

Place cleaned dried fruit in bowl with the grated carrot and apple. Add dry ingredients, grated Suenut and rind and juice of lemon. Stir in orange juice, cover and leave overnight.

Next day, add the whisky if you are using it, or a little more juice if necessary. Place mixture in two greased pudding basins, cover with greaseproof paper or cloth and steam for 8 hours.

On Christmas day, steam again for 2 hours, turn out and serve. Each pudding should serve 6-8 people.

FIG COMPOTE

8 oz (230g) figs
4 oz (120g) raisins
1 orange

2 oz (60g) almonds or
   cashews, chopped
1 tablespoon brown sugar

Wash figs thoroughly in hot water and place in dish with raisins. Add the juice of the orange and the sugar, dissolved in enough water to cover the fruit. Cover and leave overnight. Just before serving, top with the chopped nuts.

FIG PIE

12 oz (340g) shortcrust
   pastry (as for Bakewell
   Tart, doubled)
8 oz (230g) figs
2 oz (60g) raisins

2 teaspoons cornflour
1 tablespoon brown sugar
2 teaspoons lemon juice
$\frac{1}{2}$ teaspoon mixed spice

Grease a pie plate and line with just over half the pastry. Roll out rest for lid. Wash the figs thoroughly in hot water, then simmer them gently with enough water to cover until tender. Stir in the sugar and lemon juice

Make a thin paste with the cornflour and stir it in. Boil for a minute and add the spice and raisins. Cool slightly then pour into pie plate and cover with pastry. Cut slits for steam to escape.

Bake at 400°F — Mark 6 for 30-40 minutes until turning brown.

FLAMED PEACHES

4 large ripe peaches
3 oz (90g) margarine
3 oz (90g) brown sugar

4 tablespoons orange juice
2 tablespoons brandy

Melt margarine in a shallow pan, add sugar and stir to dissolve. Add juice, then the skinned, halved peaches. Turn the peaches over a low heat for a few minutes, then place them on a warmed serving dish.

Add the brandy to the juice in the pan, heat and ignite it. Pour at once over the peaches and serve.

FRESH FRUIT SALAD

3 apples
2 pears
3 bananas
4 oz (120g) grapes

rind and juice 1 lemon
2 tablespoons brown
    sugar

Place sugar in pan with ½ pint (300ml) water and heat gently until dissolved. Stir in lemon rind and juice and cool. Peel apples, pears and bananas and slice thinly into serving dish. Pour the liquid over them and scatter the grapes on top. The liquid should nearly reach the top of the fruit. Cover and chill for a couple of hours before serving.

The fruits in this recipe can be varied in season; I have used fruits which are available throughout the year.

FRUIT AND NUT DESSERT

8 oz (230g) stoned dates
2 oz (60g) ground almonds
2 oz (60g) chopped nuts

2 oz (60g) raisins
¼ pint (150ml) orange juice

Chop the dates and mix with all the other ingredients, adding more juice if necessary to make a fairly stiff mixture. Press into a bowl to give shape, turn out and serve cold.

FRUIT AND NUT JELLY

1 can orange juice
  (approximately 1 pint
  (550ml))
2 oz (60g) roughly
  chopped nuts

1 tablespoon sugar
  (optional)
2 teaspoons agar-agar or 2
  tablespoons cornflour

Heat juice and sugar in pan. If using cornflour, blend it with a little juice, stir it in and boil for a minute, stirring all the time. If using agar-agar, sprinkle it over the boiling juice and stir well until it has completely dissolved. Remove from heat and cool a little. Stir in the nuts and leave in a cool place to set.

Agar-agar will give a real jelly, so a mould may be used, but cornflour will not set so well, so it is best to leave it to set in a serving dish.

FRUIT JELLY

8 oz (230g) apricots
2 bananas
rind and juice 1 lemon

2 tablespoons brown
  sugar
2 teaspoons agar-agar

Wash and stone the apricots and stew slowly with the sugar and water to cover well. Spoon apricots into a serving dish with the sliced bananas.

Sprinkle the agar-agar over the juice in the pan whilst it is boiling and stir vigorously until dissolved. Add the lemon rind and juice and pour over the fruit in the dish. Leave to set.

MINCEMEAT FRITTERS

8 oz (230g) vegan
  mincemeat (see p. 97)
2 oz (60g) soft
  breadcrumbs

1 tablespoon lemon juice
2 oz (60g) gram flour (see
  p. 132)
oil for frying

Sift gram flour and mix to a thick batter with cold water. Stir in other ingredients. Heat oil and fry spoonfuls of the mixture on both sides. Drain and serve piping hot.

NUTTY BAKED PEARS

4 large pears
3 oz (90g) almonds,
 chopped fine
½ teaspoon almond essence

1 oz (30g) margarine
½ pint (300ml) orange,
 grapefruit or grape
 juice

Peel, halve and core pears. Melt the margarine and add the almonds and essence. Fill the pear cavities with this mixture. Place in an ovenproof dish and pour the juice over. Bake at 350°F — Mark 4 for 30 minutes. This can be eaten cold but is superb when hot.

NUTTY PEACHES

4 large peaches
2 oz (60g) chopped
 almonds or cashew nuts
1 tablespoon melted
 margarine

2 tablespoons brown
 sugar
½ teaspoon cinnamon
 powder

Halve and stone the peaches. Brush the halves with some of the margarine and mix the rest with the nuts. Fill the peach cavities with the nuts. Mix the sugar and cinnamon and sprinkle on top. Grill for about 10 minutes, keeping well away from flame or element.

Alternatively, place in an ovenproof dish and bake at 325°F — Mark 3 for 30 minutes.

ORANGE AND NUT DESSERT

4 oranges
2 oz (60g) chopped,
 roasted almonds

2 oz (60g) dates
1 oz (30g) raisins
¼ (130ml) pint orange juice

Peel the oranges and slice them into thin slices. Chop the dates. Combine all the ingredients and chill before serving.

PANCAKES

4 oz (120g) 81% flour
1 oz (30g) soya flour
1 oz (30g) gram flour
3 tablespoons oil

½ pint (300ml) water
lemon juice and sugar to
serve

Sift flours and add water slowly, beating, or liquidize together. The amount of water used will depend on the flour. Allow to stand for some time, and add 2 teaspoons of oil before cooking.

Heat a little oil in a thick pan. When really hot, pour in some batter and quickly tilt the pan so that the batter spreads out. Cook until golden brown, then turn and cook other side.

Serve as soon as possible, spreading sugar and lemon juice on one half of each pancake and folding the other half over.

PEACH SALAD

4 large peaches
½ pint (300ml) sparkling
   white grape juice

2 tablespoons sugar,
   ground fine

Peel and slice the peaches and place in individual serving bowls. Sprinkle some sugar over each bowl and pour over the grape juice. Allow time for flavour to develop before serving.

PEAR AND ORANGE PUDDING

5 oranges
3 pears
1 oz (30g) margarine

2 tablespoons brown
   sugar

Stir sugar and margarine in pan over low heat until sugar has dissolved. Add the juice from 1 orange. Slice the other orange, having first either peeled them or washed them well.

Place a layer of orange slices in a greased ovenproof dish, cover with a layer of peeled, sliced pears, and top with the remaining orange slices.

Pour the sugar mixture on top, cover and bake at 350°F — Mark 4 for 30-40 minutes. Serve hot or chilled.

PINEAPPLE FRUIT SALAD

1 large pineapple
2 oranges
2 pears
4 oz (120g) white grapes
1 peach

4 oz (120g) cherries or
    raspberries
3 tablespoons sugar
4 tablespoons lemon juice

Cut pineapple in half lengthways, discard hard centre and remove and chop flesh, reserving the juice that runs out. Peel and chop the oranges, pears and peach and stone the grapes and cherries.

Combine all the fruit in a bowl, add the sugar, lemon juice and reserved pineapple juice. Cover and chill.

To serve, spoon into the pineapple shells if liked.

PLUM SPECIAL

1 lb (450g) red plums
4 tablespoons redcurrant
    jelly

8 fl. oz (250ml) red grape
    juice or wine
1 orange

Simmer the juice for 5 minutes, add the jelly and grated rind and juice of the orange. Halve and stone the plums and place round side down in the pan. Cook very gently for 10 minutes. Place plums carefully in serving dish and pour over the liquid. Serve hot or cold.

QUICK APRICOT CHARLOTTE

1 lb (450g) fresh apricots
    (or a large size can)
3 tablespoons brown
    sugar

6 oz (180g) wholemeal
    breadcrumbs
3 oz (90g) margarine
1 teaspoon cinnamon

Fry the crumbs in the margarine until brown, then add 1 tablespoon of the sugar. Wash and stone the apricots and simmer with the rest of the sugar and a little water.

Cool slightly and liquidize or sieve with the cinnamon, keeping a couple of halves for decoration. If using canned fruit, omit the rest of the sugar and most of the syrup from the can.

Place layers of the fruit purée and the crumbs in a serving dish, finishing with crumbs and decorating with the reserved apricot halves. Serve cold.

RED FRUIT DESSERT

1 lb (450g) fresh
  redcurrants,
  raspberries or
  strawberries
1 oz (30g) sugar

2 level tablespoons
  arrowroot
2 tablespoons flaked
  almonds

Cook prepared fruit in pan with 3 tablespoons water for a few minutes until fruit has softened. Press through sieve and return to pan.

Add sugar and arrowroot, mixed to a paste with a little water. Bring to simmering point, stirring well, remove from heat and cool slightly.

Pour into serving dish and chill for at least 2 hours before serving garnished with the flaked almonds. A little Nut Cream (p. 111) or Delice goes very well with this dish.

RHUBARB CHARLOTTE

1 lb (450g) rhubarb
6 oz (180g) wholemeal
  breadcrumbs
2 oz (60g) margarine
4 tablespoons brown
  sugar

1 orange
2 teaspoons lemon juice
$\frac{1}{2}$ teaspoon ginger
$\frac{1}{4}$ teaspoon cinnamon
$\frac{1}{4}$ teaspoon nutmeg

Melt margarine and mix with crumbs. Wash the rhubarb, cut in 1-inch lengths and place in a pan with the sugar, spices, juice, rind and juice of the orange and a very little water. Heat very slowly until all the ingredients are blended, but not cooked.

Place a layer of crumbs in an ovenproof dish, add half the rhubarb and repeat the layers, reserving plenty of crumbs for the top.

Bake at 400°F — Mark 6 for about 30 minutes. Serve hot.

RHUBARB SPECIAL

1 lb (450g) rhubarb   1 orange
6 oz (180g) sugar

Wash rhubarb and cut in 1-inch lengths. Place in ovenproof dish and add the juice of the orange and the sugar. Cover and leave overnight. Next day, bake at 325°F — Mark 3 for about 40 minutes, or until tender.

RICE PUDDING

1 pint (550ml) soya milk   3 cloves
1½ oz (45g) pudding rice   ¼ teaspoon cinnamon
2 oz (60g) sugar   ¼ teaspoon nutmeg

Place dry ingredients in a greased ovenproof dish. Pour on the soya milk and cover. Bake at 300°F — Mark 2 for 2-2½ hours, removing cover for last half hour. Try replacing the spices with a couple of ground cardamoms for a change in flavour.

SAKAR PARAS

4 oz (120g) sugar   1 oz (30g) ground almonds
½ pint (300ml) water   2 oz (60g) margarine
2 teaspoons rosewater   3 tablespoons oil
4 oz (120g) 81%   1 teaspoon almond
  self-raising flour   essence

Place sugar and water in pan. Heat slowly to dissolve sugar, then boil for 10 minutes. Add the rosewater. Place flour and almonds in bowl, add melted margarine and essence and bind with a little water if necessary.

Cut this dough into sugar-lump sizes or roll into small balls and fry them in the oil until golden brown on all sides. Drain, place them in the syrup for a minute, then place in a shallow serving dish.

When all are done, pour the remaining syrup over them, cool and serve.

SPECIAL APPLE CHARLOTTE

3 cooking apples	2 tablespoons lemon juice
3 tablespoons vegan mincemeat	6 oz (180g) wholemeal breadcrumbs
3 tablespoons brown sugar	3 oz (90g) ground almonds
	2 oz (60g) margarine

Melt the margarine and stir into the crumbs and ground almonds. Peel the apples and cut into small slices. Grease an ovenproof dish and place a layer of the crumb mixture in the bottom.

Place half the apples, sugar and juice on this, then spoon over the mincemeat. Place another layer of crumbs, the rest of the apples, sugar and juice and top with the rest of the crumbs.

Bake for 45 minutes at 350°F — Mark 4, or until nicely brown on top.

SPICED SEMOLINA

6 oz (180g) semolina	$\frac{1}{4}$ teaspoon cinnamon
3 oz (90g) margarine	$\frac{1}{2}$ teaspoon cardamom, powdered
1 oz (30g) sultanas	
4 oz (120g) brown sugar	1 tablespoon rosewater
$\frac{1}{4}$ teaspoon clove powder	chopped nuts to garnish

Melt margarine in pan, add sultanas and semolina and fry until golden, stirring all the time. Add the spices, sugar and about $\frac{3}{4}$ pint (400ml) water. Continue to stir and cook gently until water is absorbed and semolina is tender, about 15 minutes.

Pour into serving dish, top with rosewater and nuts. Serve hot or cold.

STEAMED JAM PUDDING

6 oz (180g) 81% flour	1 teaspoon bicarbonate of soda
2 oz (60g) brown sugar	
3 oz (90g) margarine	2 teaspoons vinegar
$\frac{1}{4}$ pint (150ml) soya milk	3 tablespoons jam
1 lemon	

Gently heat milk, sugar and margarine until well blended. Cool and stir into the flour. Add rind and juice of lemon and the vinegar and bicarb, mixed together.

Place jam in bottom of a greased pudding basin, pour in mixture, cover well with greaseproof paper or cloth and steam for 1½-2 hours.

Turn out and serve with vegan custard.

STRAWBERRY ICE-CREAM

3 large, ripe bananas
4 oz (120g) strawberries
8 oz (230g) ground cashew nuts

Liquidize the strawberries, then sieve to remove pips. Liquidize the bananas, then add the sieved strawberries and ground nuts and liquidize again. If you haven't got a liquidizer, mash, sieve and beat instead.

Place in freezer compartment of fridge at coldest setting, and leave for several hours.

Raspberries, peaches and apricots can all be used in this way, though you may find that you need to add a little sugar.

STRAWBERRY WATER ICE

1½ lb (670g) strawberries
1 tablespoon orange juice
1 tablespoon lemon juice
4 oz (120g) sugar
½ pint (200ml) water

Mash or liquidize strawberries and sieve them unless you don't mind the seeds. Place sugar and water in pan and heat slowly until sugar has dissolved. Boil for 8 minutes. Cool slightly, then add the juices and strawberry pulp. Pour into shallow dish and freeze until set.

This recipe can be made using raspberries or blackberries instead of strawberries.

SUMMER PUDDING

½ loaf soft brown bread
1 lb (450g) raspberries
8 oz (230g) redcurrants
2 tablespoons brown sugar, or to taste

Prepare the fruit and simmer with the sugar and a little water until the juice runs. Grease a pudding basin and line with slices of bread. Pour in half the fruit, cover with a layer of bread, cover with the remaining fruit and top with more bread.

Place a weighted plate on top and leave overnight. Turn out and serve with Delice or Nut Cream (below). You can use other soft fruits for this dessert.

VANILLA ICE-CREAM

3 large, ripe bananas
4 oz (120g) ground nuts

1 teaspoon vanilla essence

Liquidize the bananas, add the nuts and essence, and liquidize again. Alternatively, beat very well. Place in freezer compartment of fridge at coldest setting and freeze for several hours.

NUT CREAM

2 oz (60g) cashew nuts
1 tablespoon oil
water

1 teaspoon brown sugar
(optional)

Grind nuts in liquidizer, add oil and sugar and water. Liquidize again, adding water until you achieve the consistency you require.

This makes a healthy and delicious alternative to cream. It keeps well in the fridge, if well covered.

Breads, Cakes, Biscuits and Sweets

This section is important, as those of you who have been using eggs in your cake recipes may well be wondering how to manage without them. I can assure you that most of my non-vegan friends queue up for my vegan cake recipes, which they find even more delicious than conventional cakes. Vegan cakes are also far less time and labour-consuming than ordinary cakes.

Nutritional values are increased by using wholemeal or 81% flour rather than bleached white flour. You may wish to substitute 1 oz of soya flour for ordinary flour in your recipes, because of its high protein content. Wheatgerm can be added to most recipes also. Tomor margarine is fine as a butter substitute. It is the only totally vegan margarine, which is suitable for cooking. Icing sugar can be replaced by demerara sugar ground down to a similar consistency in a liquidizer. If you do not own a liquidizer, borrow one from a friend and grind a few weeks' supply of sugar and nuts.

There are vegan sweets and chocolates on the market, but it is fun to make your own too. Kake Brand dark chocolate is vegan, as is Terry's Bitter chocolate. These can be used in all cooking recipes where chocolate is required. Plamil chocolate is a pleasant milk chocolate for vegans and can be used if preferred.

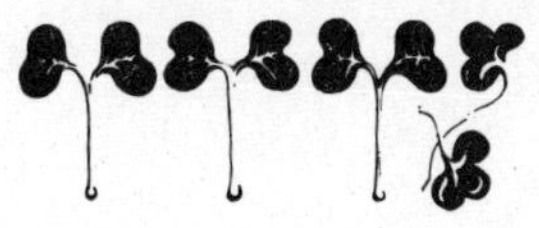 # *Breads* 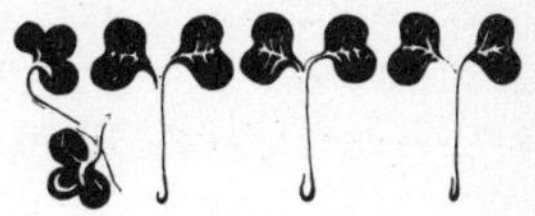

ALMOND SCONES

8 oz (230g) wholemeal
  flour
2 oz (60g) ground almonds
2 oz (60g) margarine

2 teaspoons baking
  powder
soya milk to mix

Place flour in bowl and rub in the margarine. Add the ground almonds and baking powder, then make into a stiff dough with soya milk. Roll out on a floured board and cut into rounds. Place on a greased, floured baking sheet and bake at 425°F — Mark 7 for about 15 minutes.

CORNMEAL BREAD

6 oz (180)g cornmeal
6 oz (180g) wholemeal
  flour
4 teaspoons baking
  powder

1 oz (30g) margarine
¾ pint (400ml) soya milk or
  water
½ teaspoon salt

Place dry ingredients in bowl. Melt margarine and mix it with the milk. Pour this mixture onto the flour and beat until well blended. Pour into a greased baking tin and bake at 400°F — Mark 6 for 25-35 minutes.

CURRANT BREAD

1 lb (450g) 81% plain flour
8 oz (230g) currants
1 teaspoon salt

1 oz (30g) fresh yeast
½ pint (300ml) soya milk

Place dry ingredients in bowl. Mix yeast and soya milk together and stir into the flour to make a soft dough. Knead on a floured board and leave in a warm place to rise until doubled in size. Knead once more and place in a greased 2 lb (1 kg.) loaf tin.

Bake at 425°F — Mark 7 for 15 minutes, then reduce to 375°F — Mark 5 for about 30 minutes.

DATE AND BRAZIL BREAD

12 oz (340g) 81% flour
3 teaspoons baking
  powder
½ teaspoon bicarbonate of
  soda
½ teaspoon salt
3 oz (90g) molasses

3 oz (90g) brown sugar
6 oz (180g) chopped dates
2 oz (60g) chopped Brazil
  nuts
2 oz (60g) margarine
⅓-½ pint (200-300ml) soya
  milk

Gently heat the margarine, molasses, sugar and milk until blended. Cool. Sift dry ingredients into bowl and add the dates and nuts. Stir in the liquid, adding enough milk to give a fairly soft dough. Turn into a greased, floured 2 lb (1 kg.) loaf tin and bake at 325°F — Mark 3 for 1 hour or a little longer.

MALT BREAD

1 lb (450g) 81% plain flour
6 oz (230g) malt extract
4 oz (120g) brown sugar
2 oz (60g) margarine
4 teaspoons baking
  powder

½ teaspoon salt
8 oz (230g) sultanas or
  currants
½ pint (300ml) soya milk or
  water

Gently heat the margarine, malt and sugar. Cool. Sift dry ingredients into bowl and stir in the malt mixture and soya milk. Add the dried fruit. Turn into a greased, floured 2 lb (1 kg.) loaf tin and bake at 325°F — Mark 3 for 1½ hours.

MIXED FRUIT LOAF

1½ teaspoons baking
  powder

1 teaspoon bicarbonate of
  soda

12 oz (340g) 81% flour
1 teaspoon mixed spice
1 lb (450g) mixed dried
  fruit

8 oz (230g) brown sugar
4 oz (120g) margarine
1 teaspoon vinegar
8 fl. oz (250ml) soya milk

Gently heat margarine, sugar, vinegar and milk until blended. Sift dry ingredients into bowl and add fruit. Stir in cooled liquid and mix well. Place in greased, floured 2 lb (1 kg.) loaf tin and bake at 350°F— Mark 4 for 1 hour and then at 325°F— Mark 3 for about 1 hour more.

SULTANA BUNS

12 oz (340g) wholemeal
  self-raising flour
6 oz (180g) sultanas

2 oz (60g) margarine
1 teaspoon salt
soya milk

Place flour and salt in bowl and rub in the margarine. Add the sultanas and mix to a soft dough with soya milk. Mould into required shapes and place on a greased baking sheet. Bake at 375°F —.Mark 5 for 10-15 minutes.

WHOLEMEAL BREAD

1 lb (450g) wholemeal
  flour
1 teaspoon salt
1 teaspoon dried yeast

1 teaspoon brown sugar
12-15 fl. oz (350-400ml)
  warm water

Place sugar in a small bowl, add ¼ pint (130ml) of the warm water and sprinkle on the yeast. Cover and leave in a warm place for 15 minutes. Place flour and salt in mixing bowl, pour on the yeast liquid and stir. Add rest of warm water until you have a fairly soft dough.

Place in a warmed, greased 2 lb (1 kg.) loaf tin. Cover loosely with a clean cloth and leave in a warm place until risen to top of tin. This could take 30-60 minutes.

Remove cloth, dust with flour and bake at 400°F —.Mark 6 for 40 minutes. Remove from tin after a couple of minutes and place upside down to cool.

Cakes

CHOCOLATE CAKE

9 oz (260g) 81%
  self-raising flour
1 oz (30g) cocoa powder
5 oz (150g) brown sugar
4 fl. oz (100ml) oil
10 fl. oz (300ml) water

2 teaspoons baking
  powder

Filling:
3 oz (90g) margarine
5 oz (150g) brown sugar
1 tablespoon cocoa

Gently heat water, oil and sugar until the sugar dissolves. Cool.
Sift dry ingredients into bowl and add liquid, stirring well. Turn
into greased, floured sandwich tins and bake at 350°F — Mark 4
for about 20 minutes.

To make filling, cream the margarine and sugar. Dissolve the
cocoa in a little water and beat in. When the cake is cool, sandwich
it with this mixture. You can double the quantity of filling and use
it to ice the cake if you like. Or try spreading on a little smooth jam
and grating dark chocolate over it.

CHOCOLATE CRUMB CAKE

2 oz (60g) margarine
2 oz (60g) brown sugar
1 tablespoon treacle
2 oz (60g) cocoa
3 oz (90g) soft brown
  breadcrumbs
3 oz (90g) cornflakes

3 oz (90g) dark chocolate
1 oz (30g) chopped nuts
few drops vanilla, rum or
  almond essence
1 tablespoon finely
  chopped nuts for
  garnish

Melt margarine, sugar, treacle and cocoa over gentle heat until well blended. Remove from heat and stir in crumbs, cornflakes, nuts and essence. Turn into a shallow greased dish or cake tin and spread out evenly.

When this mixture has cooled, melt the chocolate in a bowl over hot water and spread it on the top. Sprinkle the finely chopped nuts over the chocolate. Leave overnight or for several hours before cutting.

CHRISTMAS CAKE

1 lb (450g) wholemeal
  flour
8 oz (230g) raisins
8 oz (230g) sultanas
4 oz (120g) candied peel
  (or glacé cherries),
  chopped
2 oz (60g) chopped
  blanched almonds
  (optional)

8 oz (230g) currants
7 fl. oz (200ml) oil
8 oz (230g) sugar
1 tablespoon molasses
$\frac{3}{4}$ pint (420ml) water
1 teaspoon baking powder
1 teaspoon bicarbonate of
  soda
$\frac{1}{2}$ teaspoon cinnamon
$\frac{1}{2}$ teaspoon nutmeg

Gently heat oil, water, sugar and molasses until sugar dissolves. Cool. Sift flour, spices, soda and baking powder into a large bowl. Stir in the liquid, then fold in the dried fruit, which should first be rolled lightly in a little flour. Add more water if the mixture seems too dry, though it should be fairly stiff.

Turn into a greased 9-inch cake tin and bake at 300°F — Mark 2 for 2 hours, then at 250°F — Mark $\frac{1}{2}$ for about 1$\frac{1}{2}$ hours. To prevent the top burning, place a sheet of greaseproof paper over the cake tin for the last 1$\frac{1}{2}$ hours.

When cake has cooled, store in a tin until you are ready to ice it.

COFFEE SANDWICH CAKE

10 oz (290g) 81%
  self-raising flour
4 oz (120g) brown sugar
4 fl. oz (100ml) oil
10 fl. oz (300ml) water

1 tablespoon instant
  coffee
2 teaspoons baking
  powder

Filling:

3 oz (90g) margarine
5 oz (150g) brown sugar

1 tablespoon instant
coffee

Gently heat oil, water and sugar until sugar dissolves. Add the coffee, and cool. Sift flour and baking powder into bowl. Beat in the liquid and divide mixture between two greased, floured sandwich tins. Bake at 350°F — Mark 4 for about 20 minutes.

To make filling, cream the margarine and sugar and add the coffee dissolved in a little hot water. When cakes have cooled, sandwich together with this filling.

ECCLES CAKES

Pastry:

8 oz (230g) strong brown
   bread flour
7 oz (210g) margarine
pinch salt
1 teaspoon lemon juice
$\frac{1}{4}$ pint (150ml) ice-cold
   water

Filling:

1 oz (30g) margarine
4 oz (120g) currants
1 oz (30g) chopped
   candied peel
1 oz (30g) brown sugar
$\frac{1}{4}$ teaspoon nutmeg
$\frac{1}{4}$ teaspoon mixed spice

Sift flour and salt into bowl. Add the margarine in small lumps and mix to an elastic dough with the juice and water. Place on a floured board and roll away from yourself into a long strip.

Dust with flour, damp the edges and fold into three, give a half turn and roll out again. Repeat three times, resting between rollings. Roll out finally $\frac{1}{4}$-inch thick and cut into 4-inch rounds.

To make the filling, melt the margarine, stir in the other ingredients and leave to cool. Divide the filling between the pastry rounds, damp the edges and gather them together, pinching to seal. Turn over and lightly roll until the currants start to show through.

Mark with a knife, brush with water and sugar and place on greased baking sheet. Bake at 425°F — Mark 7 for 15-20 minutes.

FLORENTINES

4 oz (120g) margarine
4 oz (120g) brown sugar
4 oz (120g) blanched,
  chopped almonds
2 oz (60g) flaked almonds
2 oz (60g) glacé cherries

4 oz (120g) candied orange
  peel, chopped finely
1 tablespoon chopped
  angelica
4 oz (120g) Terry's Bitter
  chocolate

Stir margarine and sugar over gentle heat until sugar dissolves. Bring almost to boiling point and add the fruit and nuts. Remove from heat and cool. Place spoonfuls of the mixture on a greased baking sheet, leaving plenty of room for spreading. Bake at 375°F — Mark 5 for 7-10 minutes.

Let the florentines set well before carefully removing them from the baking sheet with a palette knife. Melt the chocolate in a bowl over hot water. Let it cool and work it with a knife until creamy. Just before it sets, spread it on the smooth side of the florentines. Allow to harden before serving.

FRUITARIAN CAKE

4 oz (120g) stoned dates
3 oz (90g) dried bananas
6 oz (180g) nuts, cashew,
  hazel or Brazil

6 oz (180g) raisins
1 tablespoon lemon juice
rice paper

The easiest way to make this cake is to put the fruits and nuts through a mincer. (Stops it going rusty!) Otherwise, chop the ingredients finely and knead together. Stir in the juice, and place the mixture between sheets of rice paper and cut into desired shapes.

FRUIT CAKE

8 oz (230g) wholemeal
  flour
8 oz (230g) dried fruit

3 oz (90g) Nutter or
  Suenut
5 oz (150g) brown sugar

7 fl. oz (200ml) water
½ teaspoon bicarbonate of
  soda

1 teaspoon baking powder
pinch cinnamon, nutmeg
  and mixed spice

Place sugar, water, Nutter and fruit in pan and heat gently until sugar dissolves. Then raise the heat and simmer for 5 minutes. Cool. Sift the dry ingredients and stir in the liquid.

Turn into a greased tin and bake at 350°F — Mark 4 for 1¼-1½ hours.

GINGER CAKE

10 oz (290g) wholemeal
  flour
10 oz (290g) molasses
5 oz (150g) brown sugar
1 teaspoon bicarbonate of
  soda

3 fl. oz (80ml) oil
½ pint (300ml) water
1 teaspoon ginger
3 oz (90g) preserved
  ginger (optional)

Gently heat the oil, water and sugar until the sugar dissolves. Stir in molasses and ginger powder. Sift flour and soda and stir in the liquid. Add preserved ginger, cut into small pieces. Turn into greased tin and bake at 325°F — Mark 3 for 1-1½ hours, until inserted skewer or knife comes out clean.

LITTLE SESAME CAKES

12 oz (340g) wholemeal
  flour
8 oz (230g) brown sugar
5 fl. oz (150ml) oil
8 fl. oz (250ml) water
3 oz (90g) sesame seeds

6 oz (180g) currants
1 teaspoon bicarbonate of
  soda
1 teaspoon cinnamon
½ teaspoon nutmeg

Gently heat the oil, sugar and water until the sugar dissolves. Sift flour, soda and spice into a bowl. Add the cooled liquid. Stir well, then add the seeds and currants. Turn into greased cup cake tins and bake at 350°F — Mark 4 for about 20 minutes.

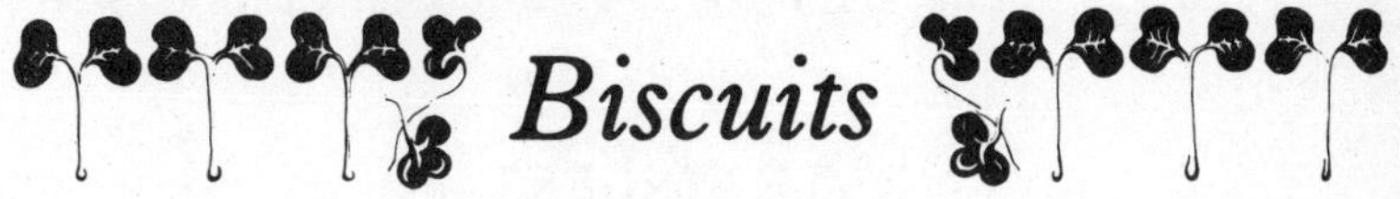

Biscuits

ALMOND BISCUITS

4 oz (120g) 81% self-
  raising flour
4 oz (120g) margarine
2 oz (60g) brown sugar

1 oz (30g) ground almonds
1 oz (30g) flaked almonds
½ teaspoon almond essence

Cream the sugar and margarine and add the other ingredients, mixing well to a stiff dough. Make balls of dough, press into rough circle shapes and place on a greased baking sheet, well spaced out. Bake at 325°F — Mark 3 for about 20 minutes. Cool on the sheet before removing.

CHOCOLATE CRUNCHIES

6 oz (180g) chopped
  almonds (or almonds
  and cashews)

1 lb (450g) dark chocolate
4 oz (120g) raisins

Melt the chocolate in a bowl over hot water and stir in the nuts and raisins. Place spoonfuls of the mixture on greaseproof paper and leave to set.

CRUNCHY BISCUITS

4 oz (120g) rolled oats
4 oz (120g) wholemeal
  flour
½ teaspoon baking powder
2 oz (60g) brown sugar

3 oz (90g) currants
3 fl. oz (80ml) oil
4 fl. oz (100ml) water
1 teaspoon mixed spice

Gently heat the oil, water and sugar until the sugar dissolves. Place the other ingredients in a bowl and pour on the liquid. Stir well until a stiff mixture. Spread out on a greased baking sheet and bake at 300°F — Mark 2 for about 40 minutes. Cut into shapes while hot.

DATE FINGERS

8 oz (230g) 81% flour
6 oz (180g) margarine
4 oz (120g) brown sugar

6 oz (180g) chopped dates
1 teaspoon baking powder

Rub the margarine into the flour and baking powder. Add the sugar and dates and knead into a stiff dough. Press into a shallow baking tin, so that the mixture is about ½-inch thickness. Bake at 325°F — Mark 3 for about 40 minutes. Cut into fingers while warm, before removing from tin.

FLAPJACKS

8 oz (230g) rolled oats
5 oz (150g) margarine

3 oz (90g) brown sugar
1 tablespoon molasses

Melt the margarine and stir in the sugar and molasses. Mix well, then add the oats. Press into a greased shallow cake tin and bake at 375°F— Mark 5 for 25 minutes. Cut into desired shapes while still hot.

FRUITY CHOCOLATE CRUNCH

2 oz (60g) muesli base
2 oz (60g) chopped
  almonds or cashews

4 oz (120g) sultanas
6 oz (180g) dark chocolate
½ teaspoon almond essence

Melt chocolate in a bowl over hot water and add the essence. Stir in the other ingredients and mix well. Place spoonfuls of the mixture in paper cases and leave to set.

GINGERBREAD MEN

8 oz (230g) 81% plain
  flour

4 oz (120g) margarine
4 oz (120g) brown sugar

2 tablespoons molasses
1 teaspoon ginger
2 teaspoons orange juice

a few currants or nuts for
decoration

Sift flour and rub in the margarine. Add the sugar, ginger, molasses and juice to make a firm dough. Roll out on a floured board and cut into shape. This is easy if you cut out a cardboard shape first, place it on the dough and cut around it.

Place the men on a floured baking sheet, adding currants for eyes and buttons. Bake at 350°F — Mark 4 for about 10 minutes. Cool on the tray.

OATCAKES

8 oz (230g) medium
   oatmeal
1 oz (30g) Suenut
$\frac{1}{4}$ pint (150ml) water

$\frac{1}{4}$ teaspoon bicarbonate of
   soda
$\frac{1}{4}$ teaspoon salt

Place dry ingredients in bowl. Bring Suenut and water to the boil and pour over oatmeal. Mix well, adding more water if necessary, to a fairly soft dough. Roll out thinly on a floured board and cut into 7-inch circles. Cut each circle into 4 and place these wedges on a greased baking sheet. Bake at 325°F — Mark 3 for about 25-30 minutes, until edges start to curl up.

OATMEAL BISCUITS

8 oz (230g) wholemeal
   flour
4 oz (120g) medium
   oatmeal
2 oz (60g) soya flour

5 oz (150g) brown sugar
4 oz (120g) margarine
$\frac{1}{4}$ teaspoon cinnamon
$\frac{1}{4}$ teaspoon nutmeg
$\frac{1}{2}$ teaspoon ginger

Combine all the dry ingredients in a bowl and rub in the margarine. Add sufficient water to make a stiff dough. Roll out on a floured board and cut into rounds. Place on a greased baking sheet and bake at 350°F — Mark 4 for 20-30 minutes.

PEANUT BISCUITS

4 oz (120g) wholemeal
  flour
½ teaspoon baking powder
3 oz (90g) margarine

2 oz (60g) brown sugar
3 oz (90g) shelled, raw
  peanuts

Cream the margarine and sugar, then add the dry ingredients. Mix well to a stiff dough and place balls of the mixture on a greased baking sheet, well spaced out. Bake at 325°F — Mark 3 for about 15 minutes. Allow to cool on the baking sheet before removing.

PISTACHIO FINGER BISCUITS

8 oz (230g) margarine
6 oz (180g) brown sugar
rind and juice of a small
  lemon

10 oz (290g) 81% plain
  flour
8 oz (230g) pistachio nuts

Cream the margarine and sugar, stir in the lemon rind, finely grated, and the juice. Sift in the flour and blend well. Cover dough and place in fridge until stiff. Make into finger lengths and roll in the chopped pistachio nuts.

Bake on an ungreased baking sheet at 400°F — Mark 6 for 10 minutes. This should make at least 36 biscuits.

SEMOLINA BISCUITS

8 oz (230g) semolina
3 oz (90g) brown sugar
4 oz (120g) margarine

½ teaspoon cardamom
  powder

Cream the margarine and sugar and beat in the semolina and cardamom. Allow to stand for 30 minutes, then shape into flat circles and place on a greased baking sheet. Bake at 350°F — Mark 4 for 30 minutes or until golden brown.

SWEET POTATO ROASTIES

1 lb (450g) sweet potatoes
2 oz (60g) pine kernels
2 oz (60g) ground cashew
  or hazel nuts

2 oz (60g) sugar
½ teaspoon cinnamon
2 oz (60g) margarine

Peel the sweet potatoes and boil until tender, drain and mash them. Stir in the kernels, chopped, the sugar and cinnamon. Roll in the ground nuts to about 8 flattened rounds. Place on a greased baking sheet and dot with the margarine.

Bake at 400°F — Mark 6 for about 15 minutes, or until they are well browned.

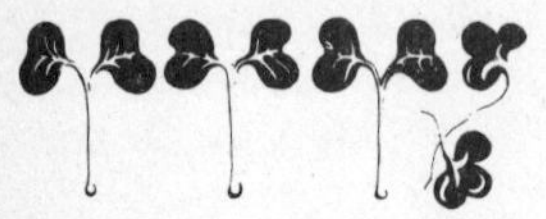 # Sweets 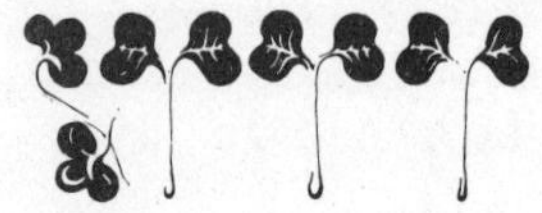

ALMOND FUDGE

8 oz (230g) brown sugar
8 oz (230g) 81% flour
2 oz (60g) ground almonds

2 oz (60g) margarine
½ teaspoon almond essence
4 fl. oz (100ml) water

Gently heat sugar and water until sugar dissolves. Boil for a minute, then add the sifted flour and cook, stirring, until thick. Add the essence and add the margarine in small pieces, still stirring all the time. When mixture starts to leave the sides of the pan, add the ground almonds.

Pour into a shallow greased dish and leave to set, cutting into squares while still warm.

BANANA HALVA

1 lb (450g) bananas
2 oz (60g) margarine
4 oz (120g) brown sugar

1 oz (30g) finely chopped
cashew nuts

Peel and slice the bananas and gently fry in the margarine for a few minutes. Remove from heat and mash. Add the sugar and 2 fl. oz (50ml) water and cook slowly until the liquid has been absorbed. Pour on to a greased dish and leave to set. Sprinkle the nuts on while still warm.

CASHEW NUT BARFI

12 oz (340g) broken
cashew nuts
8 oz (230g) brown sugar

8 fl. oz (250ml) water
1 tablespoon rosewater

Gently heat water and sugar until sugar dissolves. Raise heat and boil until a drop of the syrup forms a ball when placed on a cold plate. Chop the nuts finely or whizz quickly in the liquidizer. Add the nuts and rosewater to the syrup and stir until the mixture becomes dry.

Turn into a greased dish and leave to set. Cut into squares while still warm.

FRUITY FINGERS

4 oz (120g) seedless raisins
4 oz (120g) stoned dates
4 oz (120g) dried apricots
3 oz (90g) ground almonds

2 oz (60g) Brazil or cashew
  nuts
1 tablespoon lemon juice

Mince the fruit and nuts. Add the ground almonds and enough lemon juice to make into a stiff mixture. Spread on a sheet of rice paper and cover with another sheet. Leave to harden overnight and then cut into fingers with a knife dipped in boiling water.

NO-COOK FUDGE

12 tablespoons soya milk
  powder
6 tablespoons date spread
4 tablespoons ground nuts

2 tablespoons Tahini
1 tablespoon lemon or
  orange juice

Combine last four ingredients, then stir in the soya milk powder to make a stiff mixture, which will hold its shape. Form into balls, leave for 30 minutes and keep in fridge until required.

NUT BRITTLE

4 oz (120g) Kake Brand
  plain chocolate
$\frac{1}{4}$ teaspoon bicarbonate of
  soda

1 lb (450g) demerara sugar
8 oz (230g) ground nuts,
  almond, Brazil or
  cashew

Melt sugar in heavy pan over low heat, stirring all the time. When it has all melted, stir in the soda and nuts. Turn out on to a greased baking sheet and roll out to ¼-inch thickness. Mark into shapes before it cools.

Melt the chocolate in a bowl over hot water and spread on top of the cold brittle. Break into pieces when the chocolate has hardened.

SESAME BRITTLE

8 oz (230g) brown sugar
4 oz (120g) sesame seeds

½ pint (300ml) water

Gently heat sugar and water in a thick pan until the sugar dissolves. Bring to the boil and cook until temperature reaches 310°F. Add the seeds and pour on to a greased baking sheet. Mark into squares and leave to set.

SULTANA HALVA

1 lb (450g) sultanas
1 lb (450g) brown sugar
8 oz (230g) margarine

¼ pint (150ml) water
1 tablespoon rosewater

Fry the sultanas in the margarine until well plumped up. Remove from heat and mash. Gently heat sugar and water until sugar dissolves, then boil for 5 minutes. Add the rosewater and mashed sultanas and simmer until the syrup gets absorbed. Pour into a shallow greased dish and leave to cool, then cut into squares.

TRUFFLES

8 oz (230g) Terry's Bitter
    chocolate
2 oz (60g) Suenut
4 oz (120g) demerara
    sugar

4 oz (120g) ground
    almonds
2 tablespoons rum (or
    water and rum essence)

Grate 2 oz (60g) of the chocolate finely and keep in a plastic bag. Melt the chocolate with the rum in a bowl over hot water. Add the melted Suenut and remove from heat. Stir in the ground almonds and the sugar, which should first be pounded or whizzed in the liquidizer to a fine consistency. Mix well and leave in the fridge to cool for 20 minutes.

Roll into little balls and drop into the chocolate bag to get coated in the grated chocolate. Place in paper sweet cases and cover.

TURKISH DELIGHT

1 lb (450g) demerara sugar
¼ teaspoon citric acid
½ pint (300ml) water
1 oz (30g) agar-agar
few drops vanilla essence

few drops almond essence
1 oz (30g) cornflour,
blended with 2 oz (60g)
pounded demerara
sugar for coating

Heat the water and add the acid and sugar. Heat slowly until the sugar dissolves, then boil for 20 minutes. Slowly sprinkle on the agar-agar, stirring vigorously to prevent lumps. Add the essences and pour into a shallow greased tin. Leave to set overnight.

Sift the fine sugar and cornflour on to greaseproof paper. Turn the Turkish Delight onto the paper and cut it into squares. Toss to coat each square and place in paper sweet cases and store in an airtight tin.

Miscellany

This section is a hotchpotch of useful hints for vegans. I have come across these hints through keeping my eyes open in shops, sifting through vegetarian and vegan publications, and through experience.

Most vegans prefer to use 100% wholemeal flour in their recipes. However if this is too heavy for some tastes, 81% flour can be used. The 81% means that 19% of the bran etc. has been removed from the flour. It is still a brown flour and has nothing artificial added to it. Unbleached white flour is also obtainable from health food stores. Soya flour should be heat-treated, as the untreated bean causes indigestion. So check with your supplier before buying. Bulgur is partially cooked, cracked wheat.

If you have read all the recipes in the earlier sections you may have noticed the use of gram flour in pancakes, batters, etc. This flour is really the most useful flour for vegans, as it can replace eggs in nearly all recipes. It is made from gram (chick-peas or garbanzos) and can be bought in many health food shops and all Indian grocery stores. To use it, simply sift it and mix with cold water to the desired consistency.

Vegans often come to live happily without any milk substitute. However, at first a substitute is very helpful. I found it took me about three weeks to get used to the new taste. There are now at least four vegan milks on the market. There is a very expensive almond milk, which comes in liquid form in cans. For everyday use it is cheaper to use Granogen or Plamil. Granogen is a dried milk based on soya flour. You blend it with water before use. A baby milk version, Granolac, is also available. Plamil is the original plant milk. It comes in liquid form in tins and is diluted with an equal quantity of water before use. Delice is a thicker, sweeter version of Plamil and can be used as a cream substitute. Both Plamil and Granogen contain vitamin B12, which is important for vegans, as it is the one vitamin which is found normally only in meat and dairy produce. Recently many new soya bean milks have come on to the market, some of which contain no sugar. Where I have suggested the use of soya milk or plant milk in a recipe, any of these milks will be satisfactory.

There are many useful and nourishing items which are worth keeping in stock. Tahini, which is made from sesame seeds and tastes somewhat like peanut butter, is rich in calcium and can be spread on bread or mixed into sauces to thicken them and increase their food value. Miso is a thick paste of fermented soya and is a good foundation for soups and stock — a little strong to eat on its own. Real Tamari soy sauce is worth buying as it adds flavour to soups, stocks and sauces. Beware of cheap imitations.

There are a number of convenience foods which are useful for cooks who don't have too much .time to spend in the kitchen. There are several pleasant rissole mixes on the market, and two excellent sausage mixes, Sosmix and Sosfry. You simply add water and form into shape by hand. Another useful item is a kind of T.V.P. called Smokey Snaps. This consists of little crunchy pieces of protein with a smoky bacon flavour. It can be used to add flavour to rice dishes, or bean and vegetable casseroles. It can also be used in place of crispy bacon rashers in any of your (former) favourite recipes.

Vegetable cooking oil is useful, not just for frying, but as a substitute for butter or margarine in cake or pastry recipes. Soya bean curd or cheese can be bought from Chinese shops, where it is known as Tofu. It can also be made at home. Let your diluted Granogen milk stand in a warm kitchen for a day or two. It will thicken and can be placed in a piece of muslin suspended over a bowl overnight. Next day you should be left with a sour, creamy cheese. If you need a little yoghurt, use the soured milk without straining. For a hard cheese substitute try the following: melt 4 oz (120g) Tomor margarine and stir in slightly less than 4 oz (120g) gram flour and a teaspoon of yeast extract. Add chopped herbs if desired and leave in fridge to set.

Ghee is widely used in Indian cookery. The most expensive ghee is in fact clarified butter. However most people use the cheaper vegetable ghee which is mainly composed of palm oil. Ghee does add a distinctive flavour to Indian dishes. It is widely available in Indian grocery stores. Other fats like Cashewnutta and Nutter are nut-based and also add a special flavour to food. Suenut is a vegetable fat which can replace suet in all recipes. Recently other solid vegetable fats have become widely available in all grocery shops and may be used as suet or lard substitutes.

If you can't make your own jams and want to avoid the cheap commercial varieties with their white sugar and artificial colouring, try this recipe: liquidize equal parts chopped dates and fresh fruit. This will keep for a couple of days if covered and kept in the fridge.

I have already mentioned the necessity of nuts in the diet. Nuts are expensive, so it pays to buy in bulk. Broken cashews are often sold at nearly half price and are excellent value. Cashews and almonds can be toasted under the grill. This enhances their flavour and makes a pleasant between-meals snack. Peanuts and cashews can also be fried in a little oil. You can flavour them with salt or chilli powder.

Dates, which are an excellent sugar substitute, are expensive to buy in your local grocery store. Try to buy the not-so-lovely ones available at bulk-buy health food shops.

A liquidizer is a very useful item of kitchen equipment. Liquid or soft foods can be puréed without the tiresome bother of sieving them. Most liquidizers have an attachment for grinding nuts, or else allow the nuts to be ground in the main body of the liquidizer. It is worth checking before you begin.

A pressure cooker is extremely useful for cooking beans. In the normal way beans which have been soaked overnight may take ¾ of an hour to cook. Some types, like chick-peas, may take even longer. A pressure cooker can cut this time to 10-20 minutes.

Although vegans will patronise health food stores for their convenience foods and plant milks, it will be cheaper to buy nuts, cereals and flours from bulk-buy wholefood stores. There are now hundreds of these shops up and down the country — often located in the back streets of our towns. You can usually find these shops by looking for advertisements in 'alternative' publications and shops, or university or college campuses. Many of the weekly markets in large towns have cheap health food stalls.

Finally, I include two addresses indispensable for vegans:
The Vegan Society, 33-35, George St, Oxford, Oxfordshire.
The Vegetarian Society, Parkdale, Dunham Rd, Altrincham, Cheshire.

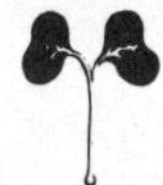

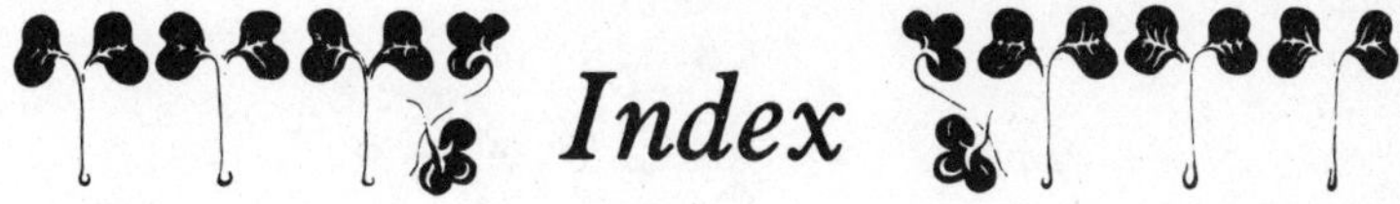

Index